Robert E. Lee

in War and Peace

The Photographic History of a
Confederate and American Icon

Donald A. Hopkins

SB

Savas Beatie

California

© 2013, 2018 by Donald A. Hopkins

Library of Congress Cataloging-in-Publication Data

Hopkins, Donald A., 1940-
Robert E. Lee in War and Peace: The Photographic History of a
Confederate and American Icon / Donald A. Hopkins.
pages cm
Includes bibliographical references.
ISBN 978-1-61121-120-7
1. Lee, Robert E. (Robert Edward), 1807-1870–Pictorial works.
2. Generals–Confederate States of America–Biography–Pictorial works.
3. Confederate States of America. Army–Pictorial works.
4. United States–History–Civil War, 1861-1865–Pictorial works.
I. Title. E467.1.L4H748 20133
55.0092–dc23
[B]
2013003600

ISBN-13: 978-1-61121-421-5
First trade paperback edition, first printing.

SB

Savas Beatie
989 Governor Drive, Suite 102
El Dorado Hills, CA 95762
Phone: 916-941-6896
(web) www.savasbeatie.com
(E-mail) sales@savasbeatie.com

Our titles are available at special discounts for bulk purchases. For more details, please contact us at sales@savasbeatie.com or call 916-941-6896.

Proudly printed in the United States of America.

DEDICATION

The youth of 16 exaggerated his age and became a young man all too quickly after enlisting in the service of his country a few years prior to WWII. During the war he found himself among other young Americans on foreign fields locked in deadly combat with a ruthless enemy—winning a Silver Star for heroism on his first day in combat. Participating in three combat jumps with the 504th Parachute Infantry, he left his mark on the enemy as one of the feared "Devils in baggy pants." However, he could not deny the scars he bore back home to Virginia, some inflicted by the enemy, some due to debilitating disease, and some possibly the result of less visible demons all too familiar to combat veterans. He was one of the finest examples of the "Greatest Generation" I have known. This book is dedicated to Walter Cecil Anderson, Jr. (1922-2012) of Halifax County, Virginia, who like me, admired the great chieftain, Robert E. Lee.

TABLE OF CONTENTS

TABLE OF CONTENTS
(continued)

TABLE OF CONTENTS
(continued)

PREFACE

This history of the photographic images of General Robert E. Lee is an unintended consequence of my lifelong interest in the Civil War period of Southern history. As a longtime collector of a broad range of artifacts associated with those dramatic times, I gradually became focused on the little visiting card-sized photographs of soldiers and notables of the era and naively began to assemble the "definitive" collection of photographs of Confederate generals. I suppose I was motivated by the same instincts that led us kids of the '50s to seek out the most famous faces for our baseball card collection. But I soon realized the futility (and expense) of my project, so I began to concentrate on pictures of only one Confederate general, the most famous of all: General Robert E. Lee.

While studying Lee's photographs and his photographers, I became aware of many mistakes in attribution, dating, and descriptions of circumstances surrounding the production of his pictures. Errors, omissions, and sheer speculation found in the earlier (1947) work by Roy Meredith, *The Face of Robert E. Lee in Life and in Legend*, sometimes found their way into more modern works by Philip Van Doren Stern, Emory Thomas, and David Eicher. Even more troublesome, I found much confusion and misunderstanding in old notes and memos accompanying photographs and negatives tucked away in many well-known archival collections. For example, in one of our national collections the "Booted and Spurred" photograph, made in 1863, which shows the General standing erect in full uniform with sword and binoculars, has a note attached saying that it was made after the war for Queen Victoria! Such a photograph actually would have been illegal at that time. Other equally prestigious archives have many examples of Lee photographs with incorrect attribution as to the original artist who made the photograph and/or the timing of the photographic sitting. From a collector's perspective, I began to notice that the descriptions of Robert E. Lee photographs as "from life" images were absolutely erroneous in all but a very few cases. This perhaps unintentional but still dishonest practice leads to

more confusion, as well as falsely inflated valuations for many of these photographs.

My initial lack of knowledge regarding early photographic techniques required that I spend some time studying the basics so that I could converse with other collectors, dealers, and archivists about daguerreotypes, tintypes, salt prints, collodion/albumen prints, and such subjects. I sifted through a multitude of books, magazines, and articles, many of which were very detailed and technically challenging. After distilling this information into a usable body of basic knowledge, I realized that the development of photography in America chronologically paralleled Robert E. Lee's adult life. The concept of a monograph that would provide examples of all 61 currently known "from life" photographs of Robert E. Lee while presenting the circumstances surrounding each photographic session gradually evolved. This study is augmented with a few paragraphs describing each of the nineteenth century photographic techniques used to make the pictures. In addition, in order to make it more useful to those interested in antique photographs in general, the book intersperses brief discussions of topics unique to photography of this period, such as revenue stamps and their usage, early photographic vignetting, blockade-run photographs, pirated photographs, early photographic enlargement, copyrights on photographs, and backmarks, to name a few. The narrative is further fleshed out with brief sketches of Lee's photographers. Many years of research, study, and analysis went into fully developing these features. The result is the most complete study of Robert E. Lee photographs available, one which is in several ways very different from prior works which purported to focus on images of the General.

In contrast to this narrative, Roy Meredith's work,—still considered by many to be the go-to reference for information about Robert E. Lee photographs—has descriptions of only 36 different photographs.[1] There is very little discussion of photographic techniques or of Lee's photographers, and virtually no mention of other associated topics. Furthermore, Meredith's book contains several errors and some glaring omissions, such as Alexander Gardner's magnificent photographs of Lee. Philip Van Doren Stern's *Pictorial Biography* (1963) places only 19 different examples of Robert E. Lee photographs among an array of images of other persons, places, and artifacts in his biographical study of the Lee family.[2] David Eicher's more recent (1997) work presents 45 photographs interspersed in what can be best characterized as another interesting pictorial and biographical study of Robert E. Lee, his family, and his surroundings.[3] Emory Thomas' *Album* (2000) leans even more heavily upon artifacts and places related to Robert E. Lee's family, with only 11 different photographs of the General himself.[4] Several erroneous assumptions seem to be carried forward into each of these later books from Meredith's study, which in turn may have been unduly influenced by Francis

Trevelyan Miller's 10 volumes of *The Photographic History of the Civil War*, published in 1912. There is very little discussion in any of these older studies of photographic techniques, photographers, or associated topics of interest to those concerned with nineteenth century photography in general.

This effort to present and discuss an example of every known photograph of General Robert E. Lee sometimes required using reproductions of halftone copies of photographs found in various old print publications rather than direct copies of original photographs, as the original photograph was no longer available. In addition, in some cases, in spite of diligent searching, an old, poor-quality photograph tucked away in an archival repository was the best example of a particular photograph that could be found. In order to present the most complete study to date of photographs of Robert E. Lee, this book uses such examples if an exhaustive search for a corresponding original photographic print in good condition was unsuccessful. I believe serious students of antique photography will understand and forgive this discrepancy. Fortunately, any photograph made before 1923 is by law in the public domain, so there are no copyright issues involving any individual examples of the Robert E. Lee portraits presented here.

I hope that this work's fresh perspective on Robert E. Lee photographs, which draws heavily on modern information-sharing technology, will be of benefit to collectors, dealers, and archivists as well as others with a general interest in nineteenth century photography.

Notes
Preface

[1] Roy Meredith, *The Face of Robert E. Lee in Life and in Legend* (New York, NY, 1981).

[2] Philip Van Doren Stern, *Robert E. Lee, the Man and the Soldier* (New York, NY, 1963).

[3] David J. Eicher, *Robert E. Lee: A Life Portrait* (Dallas, TX, 1997).

[4] Emory M. Thomas, *Robert E. Lee: An Album* (New York/London, 2000).

INTRODUCTION

"A photograph is usually looked at—seldom looked into."[1]

Robert E. Lee's face remains one of the more recognizable images of American portraiture, even though, according to his youngest son, he never relished having his photograph taken.[2] Only two known photographs of Lee date from before the Civil War, and Lee sat for photographers only five times during the entire four-year-long struggle. After the war, because of the demands of admirers both in America and abroad for current "likenesses" of the beloved general, he was photographed at as many as 15 different sessions.

The printmakers of the day, their work dependent upon accurate photographs of General Lee, were frequently frustrated because of the rapid changes in his appearance. To some his visage seemed to age 20 years during the four years of the war. At the beginning his hair and mustache were very dark, but within two years he had lost some hair and the rest was rapidly graying, as was his now-full beard. Before the end of the conflict his hair and beard were almost white.[3]

The photographs most cherished by museums and collectors are those printed directly from the original, unaltered negative that was produced as Lee sat before the camera, especially during the Civil War. "From life" photographs, in the case of this Southern icon, are quite scarce, and a true "from life" image of Robert E. Lee is an important find. Later copies of the original made from mod-

ified negatives, or altered and re-photographed photographic prints, are much more common than those rare pictures made from the original negative. Also, many later-generation copies of a particular Lee photograph are of a size different from the original negative plate.

General Lee, as a Confederate military leader, spent most of his time within Virginia (part of which later became West Virginia). The final months of 1861 he spent shoring up defenses along the Georgia and Carolina coasts, and of course he later conducted brief campaigns in Maryland and Pennsylvania. When outside of Virginia's borders during the war, he evidently had neither the time nor inclination to sit for photographs. Therefore, Virginia photographers are believed to have made all known wartime photographs of Lee, with one possible exception: an image of the General on his horse Traveller taken by an unknown photographer in Petersburg, Virginia, near the end of the war.[4]

During the last four years of Robert E. Lee's life, he had quite a few photographs taken, including several by Michael Miley (of Boude and Miley) of Lexington, Virginia, at the Stonewall Art Gallery. Lee's home at the time was in Lexington while he was serving as the president of Washington College. It is impossible to assign exact dates to each of the final few images of the aging general. In some cases even the photographer is not known for certain. In an attempt to place these images in reasonable chronological order, I consulted previous studies of the General's images along with information in archival repositories and private collections of Lee photographs. In addition, I found occasional clues scattered throughout the Lee family correspondence. Memoirs and biographies of his photographers were useful, when available. The actual appearance of the chronically ill and aging general as he appears in successive images prior to his demise in October 1870 provided some subjective information. It was also most helpful to examine descriptions in reputable auction catalogs in which his images appeared for sale, especially for images with both dated presentation notations and signatures of Robert E. Lee.

A note of explanation: the many brief sketches of General Lee's photographers scattered throughout this manuscript are arranged so that the first discussion of a photographer provides an overview of his professional career, business locations, and associates. The same photographer may be discussed farther along in the narrative in the context of a certain photograph or photographic session. Because some artists (or their associates) photographed Lee at separate sessions, sometimes many years apart, this may involve repeating some information pertaining to a photographer. However, by this arrangement information about each photograph or session will stand alone, for the convenience of those who simply seek authoritative information about specific pictures of Robert E. Lee.

Lee's lifetime (1807-1870) spanned the period from the early development of the photographic image to the dawn of modern photography. What follows in this volume is a very basic study of nineteenth century photography and those photographic artists known to have photographed Robert E. Lee, accompanying presentation of the photographs themselves.

Notes

Introduction

[1] Quote attributed to Ansel Adams, a well-known early twentieth century photographer.

[2] Captain Robert E. Lee, *Recollections and Letters of General Lee* (New York, NY, 1926), 198.

[3] Mark E. Neely, Jr., Harold Holzer, and Gabor S. Boritt, *The Confederate Image: Prints of the Lost Cause* (Chapel Hill, NC, 1987), 56.

[4] General Lee always spelled his favorite horse's name in the English manner, using two "ells."

ACKNOWLEDGMENTS

This project could not have been completed without a great deal of support and assistance from many genuine experts in the field of antique photography who were kind enough to allow me access to the archives and collections of which they were custodians. For this I am extremely grateful. The digital images presented in this study were reproduced from copies found in several of the archives, auction houses, and collections listed below.

Alabama Department of Archives and History; Arlington House, Robert E. Lee Memorial; Bob Zeller, Center for Civil War Photography, Troutman, NC; *Civil War Times Magazine*, Leesburg, VA; Cowan's Auctions, Inc., Cincinnati, OH; Dementi Studio, Richmond, VA; Donald A. Hopkins Collection, Gulfport, MS; Douglas York Collection, Virginia Beach, VA; Gilder Lehrman Institute of American History, New York, NY; Heritage Collectibles Auctions, Dallas, TX; Howard McManus, History Broker, Salem, VA; Library of Congress, Washington, DC; Library of Virginia, Richmond, VA; Mark Katz (Shaun), Gettysburg, PA; Matthew R. Isenberg, Hadlyme, CT; Mikel Uriguen Collection, Bilboa, Basque Country, Spain; Mississippi Department of Archives and History, Jackson, MS; Museum of the Confederacy, Richmond, VA; National Archives and Records Administration, Washington, DC; *North-South Trader*, Steve Sylvia, Orange, VA; Peabody Institute Library, Peabody, MA; Seth McCormick-Goodhart, Lexington, VA; Stratford Hall, Lee Memorial Association, Stratford, VA; Swann Auction Galleries, New York, NY; University of Virginia, Charlottesville, VA; U.S. Army Heritage and Education Center, Carlisle, PA; Valentine Richmond History Center, Richmond, VA; Virginia Historical Society, Richmond, VA; Virginia Polytechnic Institute and State University, Blacksburg, VA; Washington and Lee University, Lexington, VA, Leyburn Library; William and Mary University, Williamsburg, VA, Swen Library

The author is grateful to all of those who assisted with procurement of copies of photographs or with research in various archives, as well as those who kindly passed on information and advice. Certainly, in spite of my best effort, there will be a few who offered encouragement and even bits of useful information but were inadvertently omitted from the following list. For this I sincerely apologize.

Staff members of archival repositories, and others, who graciously and patiently assisted me with my research include: Ann Drury Wellford, Manager of Photographic Services, Museum of the Confederacy, Richmond, Virginia; Meghan Glass Hughes, Director of Archives and Photographic Services, and Autumn Reichartt Simpson, Research Assistant, The Valentine Richmond History Center, Richmond, Virginia; Heather Dawn Beattie, Museum Collection Manager, and Jamison Davis, Visual Resources Manager, The Virginia Historical Society, Richmond, Virginia; Diane B. Jacob, Head, Archives and Record Management, Virginia Military Institute, Lexington, Virginia; C. Vaughan Stanley,

Special Collections Librarian, Lisa McCown, Senior Special Collection Assistant, Edna Milliner, Special Collections Assistant, Seth McCormick-Goodhart, Special Collections Assistant, Leyburn Library, Washington and Lee University, Lexington, Virginia; Laura Willoughby, Curator of Collections, Petersburg Museums, Petersburg, Virginia; Nancy Barthelemy, Archivist, Peabody Institute Library, Peabody, Massachusetts; Benjamin Bromley, Public Services Archives Specialist, Earl Gregg Swem Library, The College of William and Mary; Judith Hynson, Director of Research & Library Collections, Stratford Hall, Virginia; Regina Bush, Reference Coordinator, Library, University of Virginia, Charlottesville, Virginia; and Dr. Jeffrey Willis, Director of Archives and Special Collection, Converse College, Spartanburg, South Carolina.

Among others who kindly gave valued advice and suggestions are: Paul Clancy, Norfolk, Virginia; Howard McManus, Salem, Virginia; Douglas York, Norfolk, Virginia; Edwin L. McCoy and Shirley Sydnor, Fincastle, Virginia; Jeffrey Ruggles, Richmond, Virginia; Lance Bendann, Baltimore, Maryland; Shaun Katz, son of the late Mark Katz, Gettysburg, Pennsylvania; Katherine Brown, Historic Staunton Foundation, Staunton, Virginia; Everitt Bowles, Woodstock, Georgia. Very special thanks go to Mikel Uriguen of Bilboa, Basque Country, Spain, who has assembled what is likely the most extensive collection of photographs of Civil War generals and brevet generals in the world. His assistance has been invaluable as has that of Gil Ford and Bill Jackson of Jackson, Mississippi, very talented professional photographers who rendered many of the old photographs presented in this study suitable for publication. Bob Zeller of the Center for Civil War Photography was especially helpful with his expertise on stereographic photographs and the Mathew Brady negatives. Joe McCary of Photo Response in Gaithersburg, Maryland, was able to locate one original photograph when my efforts proved to be unproductive. Dr. John O'Brien, Professor Emeritus, University of Connecticut, Storrs, was especially informative regarding Mathew Brady's postwar photographs. Don Liberto of Biloxi, Mississippi, patiently utilized his considerable talent with an impatient sitter to obtain a suitable author's portrait.

For one who is much more comfortable when deeply absorbed in historical research than when trying to exercise his very limited writing skills, the special attention this manuscript received from the publisher was a great source of encouragement. Ted Savas tactfully guided me down the pathways of his preferred literary style. Rob Ayer, my initial editor, was doggedly determined that I "get it right" and I remain indebted to him for his input. Sarah Keeney, Marketing Director, went well beyond her marketing talents to assist with the final editing changes of the manuscript. Her assistance was invaluable. Others including Lindy Gervin, (Marketing/Administrative) participated in moving this project forward. It could not have happened without them. Jim Zach's outstanding work in providing the unique layout arrangement of this somewhat complicated narrative is certainly worthy of special praise.

Throughout the several years I have been involved in this project my wife, Cindy, was always there with words of understanding and encouragement when most needed. On many occasions she had to alter her personal schedule to accommodate my prolonged research sessions in various archives and museums—she did so without complaint. Without her constant support this book would lay unfinished.

CHAPTER 1

ANTEBELLUM PHOTOGRAPHS OF ROBERT E. LEE

"Secure the shadow 'ere the substance fades."[1]

As noted in the Introduction, Robert E. Lee's lifetime (1807-1870) spanned the period from the early development of the photographic image to the dawn of modern photography. The earliest two known photographic images of Lee have always been considered to have been made as daguerreotypes.[2]

The Daguerreotype Process

In 1839, when Robert E. Lee was in his early thirties, one of the first types of photograph, the daguerreotype, was developed in France, and was introduced into the United States shortly thereafter. Samuel F. B. Morse—better known for his work with the telegraph and the Morse code—described in the *New-York Observer* a visit to his friend Monsieur Louis Daguerre in Paris on April 20, 1839. Morse wrote of the Daguerretipes [sic]: "They are produced on a metallic surface, the principal pieces about 7 inches by 5, and they resemble aquatint engravings[3] . . . not in colors. But the exquisite minuteness of the delineation cannot be conceived. No painting or engraving ever approached it." The daguerreotype was, for its time, an amazing development.

Called by some a "mirror with a memory," a daguerreotype was a positive image on a silver-plated sheet of copper. The basic process consisted of exposing a thin sheet of copper, plated on one side with silver which had been polished to a mirror-like sheen, to iodine and bromine. This created a light-sensitive coating over the thin layer of silver. When the photographic plate was exposed through the lens of a camera to a subject surrounded by light, a chemical reaction occurred on the plate. (Appendix A)

The photograph was developed by placing the exposed plate in a vapor of mercury that brought out the image on the silver-plated surface. The fragile photograph then received minimal protection from scratches and abrasions with a coat of varnish. In order to further protect it and prevent oxidation, the picture was sealed into a glass "sandwich" to form a packet, which was then placed into a small wooden or composition (thermoplastic) case. (Appendix A)

Photographic Plate Sizes

The first thin copper daguerreotype plates fabricated in France measured about 8½ by 6½ inches; this is called "whole-plate size" today. However, the actual image size was identical to the size of the exposed plate, which could be one of several other standard sizes governed by the size of the plate-holder behind the lens of the camera. Some of the early plates manufactured in the United States were even larger than whole-plate size.[4] (Appendix A)

COMMON PLATE SIZES	
SIXTEENTH PLATE	1 3/8" X 1 5/8"
NINTH PLATE	2" X 2 1/2"
SIXTH PLATE	2 3/4" X 3 1/4"
QUARTER PLATE	3 1/4" X 4 1/4"
HALF PLATE	4 1/4" X 5 1/4"
WHOLE PLATE	6 1/2" X 8 1/2"

The daguerreotype was a unique, one-of-a-kind image; each was an original. It was fixed on a metal plate, and did not involve a negative. If two copies were required, two cameras had to be set up side by side. A copy of the image could be made later only by taking a photograph of the original daguerreotype.

The image usually presents the subject laterally reversed, similar to an image in a mirror. Special reflecting lenses that preserved normal lateral orientation were available but not commonly used. To see the subject clearly, the daguerreotype had to be held at a slight angle to prevent reflection of light as from a mirror.

The quality of these relatively expensive photographs could be stunning. However, the process had its weaknesses, and by 1860 most photographers were using other, slightly less complicated techniques to produce their pictures. But in the daguerreotype's early days, even as the clear, lifelike images became more widely known, the concept was still so novel that it was considered almost magical by many who had little understanding of the technique. Consequently, photographers were sometimes asked to do the impossible. Two anecdotes reported in the *Boston Daily Advertiser* on June 28, 1853, which first appeared in the *Springfield Republican*, serve as illustrations.

NOT DEAD YET. A few days since, a man called at a Daguerreotype room in Northhampton and bargained to have a group picture taken of his family of nine persons. The next day he appeared with his family, and on the operator's 'counting noses' and making out only eight of the family, and inquiring for the ninth, he was informed that one of the sons had been dead for five years but the father thought that he could describe him so exactly, that there would be no trouble in adding him to the picture. Another funny case is told by the same 'operator.' A woman whose husband had been dead for some months, wished to have a copy 'took' of a 'picter' of her late husband, which she had in her possession, and which, she said, it was good except the eyes and she wished to know, if the 'picter' could be 'took' or copied with the addition of a brother's eyes, which she said were exactly like her late husband's and the brother could call and sit for the eyes if it could be done.[5]

Robert E. Lee's First Photograph

The first known image taken of Lee was identified only through the statement of a post-war photographer, Michael Miley of Lexington, Virginia. According to Miley, in the late 1860s one of Robert E. Lee's daughters brought an original daguerreotype to Miley to have more modern paper copies made.[6] Tradition had it that Mathew Brady of New York made the original. After Miley copied the image, somehow the original daguerreotype portrait—of Lee with one of his sons at his side—was perhaps either lost or broken, as it can no longer be found. This scenario has heretofore been accepted by most students of Lee photographs, including Roy Meredith, Philip Van Doren Stern, and Marshall W. Fishwick.

Captain Lee's U.S. Army assignments from 1841 until August 1846 consisted primarily of engineering duty at Fort Hamilton, New York,[7] and Washington, D.C., interspersed with leave time at Arlington,[8] his wife's family estate, near the U.S. Capitol.

In 1844, Mathew Brady established his daguerreotype studio in New York City. Lee would have had easy access to the studio during this period. The young boy pictured in the daguerreotype alongside his father is one of Lee's two oldest sons: G. W. Custis Lee, born in 1832, or W. H. F. ("Rooney") Lee, born in 1837; Lee's third son, Robert, was only a toddler at the time. The boy in the daguerreotype appears to be about eight, but no more than 10 years of age. Assuming that Brady did make this daguerreotype, it would have been within the first two years after he opened his New York Gallery, before Lee left for service in the Mexican War. Custis would have been 12 to 14 years old during these years, whereas his younger brother Rooney would have been seven to nine years old, which seems to approximate closely the age of the lad in the photograph. Lee, born in 1807, would have been in his late 30s, which also seems to correlate well with the formal-looking gentleman in the picture. Some serious students of Robert E. Lee photographs have suggested that this image was perhaps a daguerreotype of Robert E. Lee's older brother Sidney Smith Lee and his son Fitzhugh. Though there is a striking similarity of the appearance of Robert and Sidney Lee, the author has not been able to confirm this assertion.[9] (Appendix B)

Certainly some photographer other than Brady may have made this picture, but the ages of the subjects at least narrow down the period during which it was made—that is,

sometime between 1844 and early 1846—and Lee's army assignments serve to strongly suggest that the location of the photographic studio was in New York.

Collodion/albumen paper copy of original daguerreotype made by Michael Miley after the war. The original, one-of-a-kind daguerreotype was probably made by Mathew Brady of New York and Washington, D.C., in about 1845. Virginia Historical Society

In late August 1846, Lee was reassigned to combat engineering duty during the Mexican War, during which time his "gallant and meritorious service" resulted in advances in rank to brevet colonel.[10] After returning home from the Mexican War at the end of June 1848, Colonel Lee was assigned to duty in Washington, D.C. The day after he returned home from Mexico, he wrote to his brother, giving a playful description of his family's reaction to his changed appearance: "Here I am once again, my dear

Smith, perfectly surrounded by this Mama & her precious children, who seem to devote themselves to staring at the furrows in my face and the white hairs in my head. It is not surprising that I am hardly recognizable to the young eyes around me, perfectly unknown to the youngest. But some of the older ones gaze with astonishment & wonder & seem at a loss to reconcile what they see, to what was pictured in their imaginations. . . ."[11]

The "West Point" Image

In April 1849, Lee was reassigned to engineering duty at Fort Carroll in Baltimore harbor.[12] He remained in Baltimore until September 1852, at which time he assumed duty as superintendent of the United States Military Academy at West Point, New York.[13] He had his second photographic sitting around the time he began his new duties.

At the time of his reassignment to West Point in 1852, Lee was noted as being five feet eleven inches tall, weighing 175 pounds, and having black hair inclined to curl at the ends. His eyes were hazel brown, and his face was smooth shaven except for a black mustache.[14] He appears to be nearing his mid-forties in this portrait. The original image, either a daguerreotype or a salt print (discussed in Chapter 2) was copied later using the collodion/albumen silver technique (discussed in Chapter 2) to print the photograph on paper. These "second-generation" photographs were copied and recopied multiple times, usually altered or "enhanced," and widely sold during the early years of the Civil War. After the war, Michael Miley of Lexington, Virginia, also made copies of this so-called "West Point" image. The original photograph can no longer be found.

From September 1852 until March 1855, Colonel Lee's duties compelled him to be at the

Military Academy on the Hudson River, with an occasional official trip to the cities of New York or Washington, D.C., Mathew Brady had opened a studio in Washington in 1849. Lee also spent some leave time at Arlington, in close proximity to Alexandria, Virginia. The original photograph could have been made in Alexandria just as well as in Washington or New York City or even West Point. At the time of his transfer to the

Collodion/albumen paper copy of the "West Point" daguerreotype made about 1867 by Michael Miley of Lexington, Virginia. The original, one-of-a-kind daguerreotype was likely made by Mathew Brady of New York and Washington, D.C., in about 1852.
Virginia Historical Society

cavalry, a fellow U.S. Army engineer described him as "an ornament to any service, combining talent, energy, urbanity, nobleness and soldierly bearing, seldom equaled, and perhaps never surpassed."[15]

Perhaps because of the time he spent in Maryland, some students of Robert E. Lee photographs have attributed this second photograph to the Bendann Brothers' gallery in Baltimore.[16] Indeed, soon after sectional hostilities began in 1861, the Bendanns produced some of the first altered paper copies of this picture, marked with their distinctive blind stamp. However, it was 1859 before the Bendanns opened their own studio in Baltimore, seven years after Lee had left Baltimore to assume his position at West Point.[17] By this time Lee had been on cavalry duty in the west for several years. There is no convincing evidence that the Bendanns made the original "West Point" photograph. Some other Baltimore artist could have made the portrait, but there is no substantiation of that either.

One fact is clear: the first copy made of this "West Point" photograph was not by Michael Miley in his postwar studio. It was produced by an as yet unknown artist in 1861, a few months after the outbreak of hostilities, at which time altered paper copies of this photograph first appeared. In August 1861, an engraving by Alexander Hay Ritchie based on a greatly modified version of this "West Point" photograph appeared in *Harper's Weekly*.[18] This was likely around the time when such altered photographic copies first began to appear on the market.

Assuming that the original "West Point" photograph was indeed a daguerreotype, then the artist who made the first paper copy would have had the actual daguerreotype at hand. The first photographer to have the daguerreotype available to copy would be its original maker. It is certainly reasonable to consider that the innovative Mathew Brady used the collodion/albumen silver process to make the first paper copy of this image. He could even have done this before turning over the original daguerreotype to Colonel Lee. Brady was one of the earliest American photographers to use the new techniques for printing photographs on paper, and he did market this pose later in a small albumen silver format, but only a few copies are known.

The traditional attribution of an original daguerreotype to Mathew Brady may be correct, but there is another, equally likely possibility as to which artist made the first albumen silver print from the original daguerreotype. The Bendann brothers, Daniel and David, operated a gallery in Richmond in 1856-57, before relocating to Baltimore. Versions of the albumen silver copy print which appeared in 1861 bearing their Baltimore imprint were some of the first on the market. The Lee family certainly could have arranged for an original daguerreotype to be photographed at the Bendann brothers' gallery while the brothers were in Richmond, and if this was the case the Bendanns would have had a glass-plate negative available to work with at the start of the war.

Whether Brady, the Bendanns, or some other artist made the original paper copies of the daguerreotype, many retouched photographic and engraved versions of this image were made and distributed early in the Civil War.

Notes

Chapter 1: Antebellum Photographs of Robert E. Lee

[1] Flowery language found in an advertisement in Richmond, Virginia, newspapers placed by a photographic gallery in 1841, when photographic portraits were just beginning to replace painted portraits of family and loved ones. Lawrence A. Kocher and Howard Dearstyne, *Shadows in Silver: A Record of Virginia,*

1850-1900, in Contemporary Photographs Taken by George and Huestis Cook, With Additions from the Cook Collection (New York, NY, 1954), 249.

[2] Robert E. Lee was born on January 19, 1807, at Stratford, Virginia, the fourth child of Revolutionary War hero Henry "Light Horse Harry" Lee and Ann Hill Carter Lee.

[3] An aquatint print was made by coating a metal plate with resin, then exposing each portion of a design etched on its surface to an acid bath for intervals controlled by the artist. The exposure to acid brought out the desired tones, usually somewhere between white and black.

[4] W. I. Lincoln, ed., *The Photographic Times* and *American Photographer*, Vol. XIX, No. 403 (New York, June 7, 1889), 279-281.

[5] *Boston Daily Advertiser* on June 28, 1853.

[6] Meredith, *The Face of Robert E. Lee*, 16. A copy of Miley's negative can be found in the Miley Collection at the Virginia Historical Society.

[7] Fort Hamilton was located near New York City. In 1841 Lee was assigned the duty of improving the defenses of the 16-year-old fort. He served as post engineer until 1846.

[8] Lee's father-in-law (George Washington Parke Custis) died in 1857, leaving his Arlington estate to Lee's wife. As customary for the times, Lee managed the estate as though it was his own.

[9] Dr. John O'Brien, Charles Town, WV, telephone conversations 9/23/2012 and 9/27/2012.

[10] Charles B. Hall, comp., *Military Records of General Officers of the Confederate States of America* (1898; reprint, Austin, TX, 1963), 1. Officers might be awarded brevet rank as recognition for gallantry or meritorious service as happened to Robert E. Lee for his Mexican War service. A brevet officer would receive pay commensurate with his brevet rank.

[11] Robert E. Lee to Sidney Smith Lee, June 30, 1848, call no. GL09257, the Gilder Lehrman Institute of American History, New York, NY. http://www.gilder-lehrman.org/collections

[12] Fort Carroll in the middle of the Patapsco River was part of Baltimore's defenses. Brevet-Colonel Lee was assigned to design the structure and supervise the construction in 1848.

[13] The Superintendent of West Point had duties much like a chancellor in modern day universities, coupled with student counseling duties. He usually had no classroom assignment.

[14] John William Jones, *Life and Letters of Robert E. Lee: Soldier and Man* (New York, NY, 1906), 71.

[15] Everard H. Smith, "As They Saw General Lee," *Civil War Times Illustrated*, Oct. 1986, 20.

[16] William P. Trent, "Robert E. Lee," in Francis Trevelyan Miller, ed., *The Photographic History of the Civil War: Thousands of Scenes Photographed 1861-65, with Text by many Special Authorities*, 10 vols. (New York, NY, 1912), vol. 10, 55.

[17] Lance Bendann, *History* (of Bendann's Art Gallery). http://www.bendannartgalleries.com/BendannHistory.htm

[18] Meredith, *The Face of Robert E. Lee*, 27. Alexander Hay Ritchie (1822-1895) a Scot, was an engraver and painter who established himself in New York in 1841. A copy of his original engraving of Robert E. Lee in the author's collection measures 3" x 6."

CHAPTER 2

CIVIL WAR PERIOD
PHOTOGRAPHY

"Perhaps in no branch or department of art, discovery or invention have the developments been so rapid and astonishing as in that of photography."[1]

After 1839, when the mirror image of the daguerreotype was introduced into the United States from France, the development of photographic techniques made steady progress. Within a few years, as the popularity of the daguerreotype declined, two other techniques came into vogue. At the start of the Civil War, the most common photographs were one-of-a-kind positive images on glass or black-painted sheet-iron plates which had been made light sensitive with chemicals. These images, like daguerreotypes, were usually encased in glass-covered, fold-open, wooden or thermoplastic cases. The images on glass were called ambrotypes; the images on sheet iron were generally called tintypes.

The Ambrotype Process

Although ambrotype images somewhat resemble daguerreotypes, the method for producing the former, developed in 1851, was very different.

Ambrotypes required the photographer to prepare a light-sensitive glass plate just prior to its exposure in the camera. A very thin, smooth, glass plate was carefully cleaned before being covered with a thick, sticky solution of an explosive mixture containing nitrocellulose called collodion. The plate was then immersed in a bath of silver nitrate, which made it light-sensitive. Once the wet collodion layer was made light-sensitive, the areas exposed to light would develop into a negative image. While still damp, the glass plate, enclosed in a light-tight plate holder, was placed behind the lens of the camera for

an exposure that ranged from several seconds to a few minutes. The somewhat underexposed plate was removed from the camera and allowed to develop. It was then rinsed off and chemically fixed to stop the development process. When dry, the negative was varnished to give some protection to the easily abraded collodion layer.

When this thin, underexposed glass negative was placed in front of a dark background, the image appeared as a positive. This is because the silver particles remaining in the negative's surface reflect light, while the exposed areas, which had no silver at all, appear black. This is the principle behind the ambrotype process.

This photographic technique, like the daguerreotype method, also produced only a single, laterally reversed image, but it was less expensive and needed less exposure. Ambrotypes were very popular well into the 1880s with American photographers.

There is no known ambrotype of Robert E. Lee "from life"; however, there are a few ambrotype copies of albumen silver paper images of Lee, many of them altered or "enhanced" to show Lee in uniform. One interesting example, rather than appearing laterally reversed as expected, was re-photographed in order to restore the image to its original laterality.

The Tintype Process

The tintype, also known as a ferrotype or a melainotype, was invented in France in 1853, and by 1856 the technique was patented in the United States.[2] It quickly became very popular as the least expensive way to make a photograph.

A tintype was made the same way as an ambrotype, except that a thin piece of black enameled ("japanned") iron was used in place of a glass plate with separate black background. Like the daguerreotype and the ambrotype, the image was also a unique image that appeared reversed laterally. Tintypes could be made in many sizes. Standard photographic plate sizes during the Civil War period generally remained the same as for the daguerreotype. Occasionally a photographer would use a camera that could accommodate a plate holder larger than whole-plate size, but this was not a common practice, particularly in the Confederacy.

There are only two known tintype images "from life" of Lee, and both are postwar pictures of the General on his war-horse. A few tintypes do exist of him, which are simply photographic copies of collodion/albumen process images, and therefore the copies appear reversed laterally from the original.

Cameras with more than one lens with each having a removable cap, or cameras with a rotating lens, or with a sliding back, were designed to expose only small portions of a single photographic plate at a

A laterally reversed copy of an early war alteration of Lee's "West Point" photograph was re-photographed as an ambrotype, restoring correct lateral orientation. Virginia Historical Society

Tintype copy of wartime photograph of Robert E. Lee. Hand-tinted by an unknown artist. Museum of the Confederacy

time. These "multiplying cameras" were developed in the mid-1800s. Many essentially identical tintypes could be made on a single thin sheet-iron plate by use of such a camera. Shears were then used to separate the individual photographs. Portraits as small as ¾ inch by 1¼ inches became common. These tiny ¹⁄₁₆ plate-size pictures were called "gem-size" photographs.

The early photographic techniques which produced daguerreotypes, ambrotypes, and tintypes resulted in what collectors and curators now call "hard images." Each of these methods produced a single image with no negative, and therefore the photograph could only be reproduced by photographically copying the hard image. These techniques were gradually supplanted by other methods which resulted in photographs that were printed on paper from a negative.

The Salt Print Technique

A paper photographic process invented in 1840 was called the "salted paper" or "salt print" technique. This was a positive printing procedure using a negative.

The first negatives were prepared from waxed or greased paper which had been made light-sensitive by various chemicals. This flimsy negative (later replaced by a glass plate) was then placed in contact with a sheet of high-quality, somewhat thick writing paper that had also been made light-sensitive by floating it on salt water and then covering it with silver nitrate. After sunlight passed through the negative to the paper to expose the photograph, the finished print was chemically fixed, washed, and dried. Most salt prints have a matte surface because the image is actually embedded in the superficial surface fibers of the paper. When paper negatives were used, salt prints were usually less sharp than the later ones made with glass-plate negatives. Their color tones can range from reddish brown to chestnut brown, often fading to a yellow color, especially around the edges.

This particular method of printing photographs directly on uncoated paper was never as popular as the methods for producing hard images, and became even less common after the invention of collodion/albumen silver techniques. In the Confederacy, primarily because of the increasing difficulty in obtaining necessary chemicals and other materials for making collodion/albumen prints, there was a persistent interest in the less complex salt print. Civil War-period salt print copies made from collodion wet-plate glass negatives are frequently seen. Most salt prints made during the war do not have a photographer's identifying imprint on them. Those that did included some large-format copies made by George W. Minnis and

Daniel T. Cowell, and a few by Julian Vannerson, all of Richmond, Virginia.

In many cases, Southern salt-print photographs were "make do" images, very small
and mounted in the center of a rather small
card, often to conserve paper. Sometimes a
tiny negative, as small as a
gem-size   tintype,
was produced
by using
a small,

prewar
ambrotype
or daguerreo-
type camera with an
adjuster or   Small, salt-print copy of photograph that was
reducing   originally made in 1863, mounted on a small,
back. This   plain card. Howard McManus, History Broker
approach
not only conserved chemicals and paper, but
was available to those photographers who
had not yet obtained a camera suitable for
producing more modern types of photographs. Scraps of cardboard or imported bris-
tolboard were often used as supports for these
smaller salt prints. On occasion, a salt print

copy of a Robert E. Lee image surfaces, usually on a plain, unadorned card.

The Wet Collodion Negative/Albumen Silver Print Process

The wet collodion process, a rather complex technique, was introduced in 1851
in England as the first practical negative system. This was a year or so
before Mathew Brady could
have made the second da-
guerreotype of Lee.

The collodion process
required that the photog-
rapher mix chemicals and
prepare a light-sensitive
glass plate just prior to its
exposure in the camera.
A smooth, glass plate
which had been carefully
cleaned was covered
evenly with a thick collodion solution, much like
in the ambrotype process.
The sticky plate was then
immersed in a bath of silver
nitrate, which made it light-
sensitive. While still damp, the
plate was placed in a light-tight
holder which was inserted into the
back of the camera behind the lens for an
exposure that ranged from several seconds to
a few minutes. Prior to inserting the
plate into the camera, the camera
was positioned and focused on the
subject. After the photographer
took the picture by exposing the negative
plate but before the exposed plate could dry,
he removed it from the camera, allowed it to
develop, then rinsed and chemically fixed it.
When dry it was varnished, providing minimal protection to the easily abraded collodion layer. The collodion negative on a glass

plate was ideally suited for use with the albumen silver printing process, which was developed at about the same time.

The albumen silver print was invented in 1850, but was not commonly used in the United States until 1860. From that time until 1890, it was the most widespread type of photographic print. Egg white (albumen), sugar from grape juice, salt (sodium chloride), and silver nitrate were applied to the surface of thin paper to produce a light-sensitive coating. When sunlight passed through a previously exposed glass-plate negative to the surface of the sensitized paper it produced an image on the paper.

Albumen silver prints (most often simply called albumen prints today) were usually mounted on various-sized cards to prevent the thin, fragile paper from curling or tearing. However, photographs could also be purchased unmounted from most photographers.

The glass-plate negative could be used over and over. For the first time in photographic history, there was a means of inexpensively producing multiple images from a single, durable negative. This process was commonly used in the United States until about 1880, when the more convenient gelatin, dry-plate negative began to replace it.

After 1860, all known photographs of Lee "from life," both wartime and postwar, were made by the collodion negative/albumen silver paper print techniques, except for two postwar tintypes.

The Carte De Visite (CDV)

The majority of all portrait photographs of the Civil War period that survive today are in a small paper format produced by the collodion negative/albumen silver print method known as the carte de visite, commonly referred to as a CDV.

These little pictures were made by using a multiplying camera to expose a wet-plate glass negative, which was then printed out on albumen silver paper. The nearly identical thin paper photographs were then cut apart and mounted on card supports. The existence of a negative allowed for the creation of almost unlimited copies.

Small portraits of military officers, statesmen, actors and actresses, politicians, and other nineteenth century celebrities were sold by the thousands after 1860. Many can be found even today assembled as collections in old leather-covered albums. Often either the photographer or an artist working for the gallery hand-tinted and colored or otherwise embellished the little images. These pictures were so inexpensive that during the Civil War period countless soldiers, sailors, and civilians purchased multiple copies of their likenesses to share with family and friends.

Generally speaking, one can separate the early wartime cartes de visite from later ones by the thickness of the paper card stock. The

Actual-size carte de visite.
Museum of the Confederacy

earliest were on very thin cards, the later ones on slightly thicker mounts. Also, cartes de visite up until about 1863 had no border designs around the image, but later ones might have red- or gold-ruled borders, either single or double. There are exceptions, but these details are sometimes helpful in dating early photographs.[3]

Stereographic Photographs

The stereograph was another form of Civil War-period photography. This technique was manifest in the photographs taken in the field by nationally known photographers and firms such as Mathew B. Brady, Alexander Gardner, George S. Cook, and Timothy O'Sullivan.

A stereograph is simply a simultaneous double image of the same subject that, when viewed through a special viewer, appears to be one three-dimensional (3-D) photograph. Stereographs were made by a specially designed single camera with two lenses set approximately 2½ inches apart. This distance between the two lenses mimics the distance between human eyes. Two photographs were produced from very slightly different angles, then glued side by side on a rectangular card. When the card was manipulated in a sliding holder in front of a viewer with two separate lenses, a single 3-D image came into focus. The stereograph became very popular as parlor entertainment once a simple, inexpensive viewer was developed in the late 1850s.

Glass negatives of General Lee's Gettysburg headquarters, made simultaneously in a stereographic camera, that show slightly different positions of the female figure in the photographs. Museum of the Confederacy

No. 573.— Gen. Lee's Headquarters.

Original battlefield photographs from the Civil War are most commonly found today as 3-inch by 6-inch stereographic views. There are many stereo-

A somewhat later depiction of General Lee's Gettysburg headquarters, shown as stereographic views mounted on a card for viewing. Library of Congress

A Civil War-era four-lens camera for production of four cartes de visite from a single 7 x 9 inch glass plate, compared alongside a typical stereographic camera. Matthew R. Isenberg

graphic outdoor portraits of officers, but "from life" stereographic images of a person are not as common as the broader views of battlefields, forts, buildings, and encampments. Prints from two

glass-plate negatives exposed in a stereographic camera show an early view of the Mary Thompson

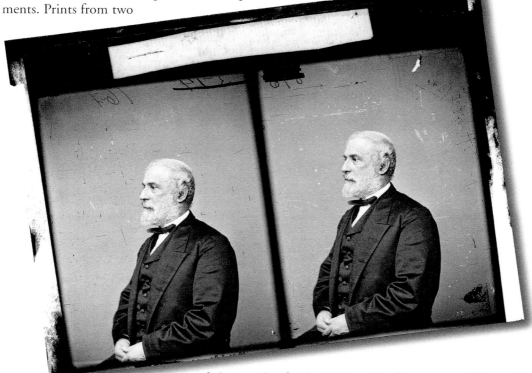

A pair of photographs of Robert E. Lee taken from a group of four made simultaneously with a four-lens camera in 1866. Library of Congress

home, which served as General Lee's head-quarters at Gettysburg. Careful examination of the position of the lady on the extreme right clearly shows that the images were made from slightly different angles.

There is no known "from life" image of Lee made with a stereographic camera. Many studio portraits, however, were taken with multi-lens cameras, and side-by-side pairs of images from those exposures are also stereo-scopic. The talented staff at the Center for Civil War Photography (CCWP) has come to rec-ognize the stereoscopic nature of side-by-side

exposures of photographs of many studio por-trait photographs made during the war.[4] When working in his gallery, in many cases, the pho-tographer used a camera with multiple lenses, usually four but sometimes three. This allowed the artist to make three or four photographic exposures simultaneously on the same negative plate. The space between the separate lenses, although not as precisely calibrated to mimic the distance between human eyes as with a stereographic camera, still allowed for enough variation in the angles of the exposures to pro-vide a stereographic effect.

Notes

Chapter 2: Civil War Period Photography

[1] John Clark, "The Photographic Art," *The Norfolk Post,* July 21, 1865. http://chroniclingamerica.loc.gov/lccn/

[2] William C. Darrah, *Cartes De Visite in Nineteenth Century Photography* (Gettysburg, PA, 1981), 2.

[3] Darrah, *Cartes De Visite*, 15.

[4] Bob Zeller, President of the Center for Civil War Photography, telephone interview, March 5, 2012.

CHAPTER 3

ROBERT E. LEE'S
WARTIME PHOTOGRAPHERS

"I believe there were none of the little things in life so irksome to him as having his picture taken in any way."[1]

Several skilled photographers were operating in Virginia, particularly in Richmond, at the beginning of the Civil War. Some moved away from Richmond prior to the war, while others relocated into the city during the conflict. Only five or six galleries were operational in Richmond at different times during the war years. In fact, the *American Journal of Photography*, reporting on photography in the South in September 1863, only somewhat understated the facts when it noted that "it is only in Charleston and perhaps Richmond that any photographs at all are made."[2]

Many of these photographers are listed in old city directories and sales tax records or referred to in newspaper ads or notices of the day. Such information is very useful when trying to determine when and where a particular artist worked. Most of the photographers mentioned in this chapter at one time or another either produced "from life" images of Robert E. Lee or sold early copies.

Photographers in antebellum and wartime Virginia changed studio locations, made new business associations, and set up branch operations on a frequent basis. It was very common for photographers of the day to share the same address or locate their gallery where another photographic salon had been previously. The reason: photographic techniques depended upon abundant sunlight, and few commercial buildings had windows with the preferred northern exposure or skylights. In multi-story buildings, the photographic gallery was necessarily on the top floor. The relatively few buildings in town suitable for a photographic gallery tended to pass from one artist to a successor in the same business.

Photographers in the
Richmond City Directory of 1860

G. W. MINNIS,	217 MAIN STREET (THE YEAR BEFORE AT 107 MAIN STREET)
E. M. POWERS,	151 MAIN STREET
C. R. REES,	215 MAIN STREET (THE YEAR BEFORE AT 139 MAIN STREET)
JOHN THOMAS SMITH,	145 MAIN STREET (THE YEAR BEFORE AT 215 MAIN STREET)[3]

The following paragraph gives a feel for the fluidity of the photography business in its early days: In 1861, A. J. Riddle from Georgia opened his gallery in Richmond at 151 Main Street, the same location that had been occupied by E. M. Powers in 1860.[4] Riddle remained until about 1864. Peter E. Gibbs was in Richmond in 1859 with an ambrotype gallery at 215 Main Street, the same address occupied later that same year by John T. Smith, and still later, in 1860, by Charles R. Rees. Gibbs was still listed in Richmond in 1860, but no occupation was specified.[5] J. H. Whitehurst owned several studios in various cities, in which he placed other photographers to operate the businesses. From about 1847 to 1855, he owned a daguerreian studio at 77 Main Street in Richmond. Prior to the war, the Vannerson brothers (Lucian, Adrian, and Julian) worked for Whitehurst at various locations, including Richmond. Before 1860, John Thomas Smith, who had been operating a gallery at 145 Main Street, evidently bought Whitehurst out.[6] Julian Vannerson joined Smith a short time later, as some large albumen photographs made about 1860 were marked "Smith & Vannerson, 77 Main Street." By early April 1861, "J. Vannerson, 77 Main Street" was found on similar photographs, suggesting that Vannerson had taken over this gallery about the time of the beginning of the war. Vannerson later made some of the most famous of the Robert E. Lee portraits. Charles R. Rees was in Richmond by mid-1859 at 215 Main Street, and in 1860 took over the gallery that had previously been occupied by Richard S. Sanxay and James F. Chalmers and later John T. Smith, all successors to William A. Pratt's operation at 145 Main Street. The building at this location was multi-story; thus, more than one business could be located at this address simultaneously.

Photography-Related Ads or Notices

Photography and the sale of photographs were competitive endeavors that led to extensive newspaper and broadside advertising. Photographic artists were not the only ones who sold photographs; publishing houses, booksellers, and other retailers offered photograph copies to the public. In March 1861, a business styling itself as "scientific and practical opticians" in Richmond posted a notice that it had received a large collection of "Stereos and Stereoviewers."[7] During the same month Vannerson's gallery was offering "Premium Photographs" at a great reduction in price, some for only one dollar.[8] During the first half of 1861, advertisements for Rees' Photographic Gallery appeared frequently in the *Daily Dispatch*.[9]

Throughout the first years of the Civil War, the large influx of Confederate troops and government officials with their families into the Confederate capital stimulated a brisk business for the local photographers. The few still working in the city, such as Julian Vannerson, were compelled to advertise for assistants.[10]

Newspaper Articles Relating to Photographers

Because of the photographic artists' stature in the business community, they were often mentioned in articles or reports in local newspapers. Fire damage was reported at Vannerson's gallery in February 1862. In July 1862, a Richmond newspaper advocated that local photographers should photograph the nearby battlefields made famous by the Seven Days battles around Richmond. In April 1865, George W. Minnis, "Daguerreotypist of Richmond," was reported to have suffered losses in the evacuation fire at the end of the war.[11]

Knowledge of when a particular photographer worked and at what address allows us to place an approximate date of origin for images which have that photographer's imprint. Fortunately, of the few photographers in Richmond in business at different times from 1861 through early 1865, four did use simple imprints, at least on their photographs intended for wide distribution. Wartime photographs, usually cartes de visite, have been identified with imprints of Vannerson, Minnis and Cowell, Rees, and Riddle. All of these men worked at some time during the war in Richmond or nearby Petersburg, Virginia. It is important to note that no wartime imprint of John W. Davies of Richmond has been found on any photograph, even though Davies has previously been credited with three well-known wartime photographs of General Lee; this matter will be discussed at greater length in a later chapter.

Imprints or Backmarks on Photographs

Many of these early photographs had addresses and logos printed on their supporting card that identified which photographic gallery made, or which publisher sold, that particular image. The earlier images bore simple names and addresses on the card mounts, but as time

An example of a typical late 1860s backmark on a carte de visite. Douglas York

passed the imprints evolved to incorporate fancy Victorian scrolls and engravings. These markings were often found on the back of the card and are now spoken of among collectors as "backmarks." On occasion a "blind stamp" was used, which was simply an inkless impression embossed into the surface, usually on the lower border of the card. These markings might indicate the photographer who actually produced the negative from a live sitting of the subject, or a photographer who, with or without permission, copied another's work. Sometimes the imprint on the photograph only identified the merchant who sold copies of the image, not the photographer.

Below is a representative, though very incomplete, list of imprints of photographers or publishers found on photographs of southern subjects. Robert E. Lee photographs have been found with each of these identifying marks, plus many others. A publishing house or other retail merchant which sold photographs often pasted their label over the backmark of the photographer who had actually made the picture. Galleries and publishers in the North also made copies of pictures of notable (or notorious) southerners during this period for sale in their market.

Imprints Commonly Found on Photographs of R. E. Lee

Anderson and Co. Photographic Art Palace, Old No. 121, New No. 1311, opposite Mitchell and Tyler's
Published by E. & H. T. Anthony, 501 Broadway, New York
Bendann Brothers Galleries of Photography, 205 Balte. St. [Baltimore]
Boude and Miley, Lexington, Virginia
Brady's National Photographic Portrait Galleries, Broadway & Tenth Street, New York and No. 352 Pennsylvania Ave., Washington, D.C.
George S. Cook, Successor to D. H. Anderson, Richmond, Virginia

George S. Cook, Artistic Photography, 913 Main St., Richmond, Virginia

H. P. Cook [Richmond, VA]

Fisher & Dennison (successor to Fisher & Bro.), Publishers and Stationery, No. 64 Baltimore St., Baltimore

C. D. Fredricks & Co., 587 Broadway, New York, 108 Calle de la Haban, Habana, 31 Passage du Havre, Paris

Alexander Gardner, 921 Penna. Ave., Washington, D.C.

Published by **F. Guntekunst** [Philadelphia, PA]

C. E. Jones and Vanerson [sic], Photographers, No. 77 Main St., Richmond, Va.

Leach & Edkins, Photographer, No. 159 West Baltimore Street, Baltimore, 1870

The Lee Gallery, 920 Main Street, Richmond, Virginia

The Lee Photographic Gallery, 920 Main Street, over the Richmond Musical Exchange, John W. Davies

Lumpkin & Thomlinson, Photographic Artists, No. 98 Main Street, Richmond, Va.

Sterling C. McIntyre, Richmond

Michael Miley, Lexington, Virginia

Minnis and Cowell, Richmond, Va. [Cartes de visite bearing an ink imprint from Minnis' studio are extremely rare, the embossed imprimatur being more common.]

G. W. Minnis, Photographic Gallery, 9th and Main St., Richmond, Va.

Monumental Photograph Co., Baltimore, Maryland

Pollock, Baltimore, Maryland

Premier Photographic Gallery, R. Wearn, Artist, 170 Main St., Columbia, South Carolina

Quinby and Company, Photographic Artists, Charleston, South Carolina

C. R. Rees & Bro., Photographers, Corner 8th and Main Streets, Opposite Spotswood Hotel, Richmond, Va.

Rees & Brother, Photographic Artists, Richmond

Rees & Company, Photographic Artists

Chas. R. Rees & Co., Photographic Artists, Richmond, Va.

J. Riddle, Photographic Gallery of Art, No. 151 Main St., Richmond, Va.

Rockwell & Cowell (Petersburg, Va.)

Rockwell & Tanner

D. J. Ryan, Savannah; sold to aid the Ladies Memorial Association of Savannah

Selby & Dulany, Bookseller and Stationers, 322 West Baltimore Street, Baltimore

W. D. Selden and George O. Ennis, Selden & Co., No. 836 Main Street, Richmond

Stonewall Art Gallery, Boude & Miley, Lexington, Va.

Vannerson, Photographic Artist, No. 77 Main St. Richmond, Va.

Vannerson & Jones, Photographer, No. 188 Main St., Richmond, Va.

Vannerson & Jones, Photographic Artists, No. 77 Main St., Richmond, Va.

Only two (or possibly three) photographers or studios are known to have made "from life" photographs of General Lee during the war. These were Minnis & Cowell, Vannerson, and possibly a third, an unknown photographer who made an outdoor image at Petersburg. John W. Davies, who has been given credit for more than 60 years for a series of wartime photographs of Robert E. Lee, did not operate a photographic studio until a few years after the end of the war.

Notes

Chapter 3: Robert E. Lee's Wartime Photographers

[1] Robert E. Lee's attitude toward having his photograph made, as stated by his youngest son. – Lee, *Recollections and Letters*, 198.

[2] James J. Broomall, "Photography During the Civil War," in Brendan Wolfe, ed., *Encyclopedia Virginia*, Virginia Foundation for the Humanities, April 12, 2011. http://www.EncyclopediaVirginia.org/Photography_During_the_Civil_War

[3] W. Eugene Ferslew, comp., *First Annual Directory for the City of Richmond to which is added a Business Directory for 1859* (Richmond, VA, 1859), n.p.

[4] Jeffrey Ruggles, *Photography in Virginia* (Richmond, VA, 2008), 28.

[5] John S. Craig, comp., "Peter E. Gibbs," in *Craig's Daguerreian Registry: The Acknowledged Resource on American Photographers 1839-1860*. http://craigcamera.com/dag/

[6] Craig, "John Thomas Smith," in Craig's *Daguerreian Registry*.

[7] Mike D. Gorman, Civil War Richmond (M.D. Gorman, 1997). http://www.mdgorman.com/Written_Accounts/written_accounts.htm

[8] Ibid.

[9] Ibid.

[10] Ibid.

[11] Ibid; Richmond evacuation fires began after midnight on April 3, 1865, as Confederate troops left the city. The fire destroyed about 35 city blocks, including several photographic establishments.

CHAPTER 4

GENERAL LEE
AS HE NEVER WAS

*"Gen'l R. E. Lee, when a Capt. of Engineers
in the U. S. Army retouched for the Memorial Church
in Lexington, Va."*[1]

No current image of Robert E. Lee was available in the marketplace at the outbreak of the Civil War. Photographers and publishers filled their orders for pictures of Lee with alterations of copies of the "West Point" daguerreotype. A carte de visite image with a Bendann Brothers, Baltimore, Maryland, backmark was perhaps the first of many artistic and photographic alterations of the early 1850s daguerreotype apparently originally made by Mathew Brady.

Some of the artistic creations were quite fanciful. Artist and engraver A. H. Ritchie created one variation by altering photographic copies of the original daguerreotype.[2] It presents Lee in the uniform of a Virginia colonel—a rank he never held. This alteration was then photographed in Baltimore by the Bendann Brothers Studio. In point of fact, Lee was a major general and commander of the Virginia forces from April until August of 1861, at which time he was promoted to brigadier general of the Confederate States, the highest rank allowed in the Provisional Army of the Confederate States at the time.

The Bendann Brothers

Many artists created versions with minimal enhancement of the daguerreotype, such as simply adding a military emblem to his hat and making his brass buttons more prominent. Examples of each variation were found in the Bendann Brothers' published album.[3]

Daniel Bendann and his younger brother David were born in Germany but came to Richmond, Virginia, as children and remained Southern sympathizers as adults. As early as 1843, Daniel was employed in the Whitehurst gallery in Richmond, and in about 1854 he moved to Baltimore to work in Whitehurst's gallery there. He returned to Richmond to open his own gallery in 1856.

Daniel again left Richmond for Baltimore in 1859, along with his younger brother David. The brothers opened their gallery at 205 Baltimore Street, where they remained until 1862, specializing in portraiture and visiting cards. They then moved to 207 Baltimore Street, where they operated their studio from 1863 until 1872.

A Bendann Brothers of Baltimore, Maryland, early wartime carte de visite showing extensive alteration of Lee's "West Point" photograph. Donald A. Hopkins

A Bendann Brothers of Baltimore, Maryland, early wartime carte de visite showing minimal alteration of Lee's "West Point" photograph. Donald A. Hopkins

During Baltimore's occupation by Federal troops, the Bendanns fell under suspicion of being Confederate sympathizers. In 1862, David was arrested and imprisoned for three months for "uttering treasonable language" and refusing to take the oath of loyalty to the Union.[4]

The Bendanns dissolved their partnership in 1872, with Daniel continuing in photography and David pursuing his interest in fine arts. The Bendann gallery was located at various points in Baltimore after that time, and still exists as the Baltimore area's oldest art gallery. According to David's great-grandson Lance Bendann, who now runs the gallery in a suburb of Baltimore, they had a wide product line, and actually patented something called a

"Bendann Background," by which they could superimpose a portrait taken in a studio onto another background. They marketed negatives of various backgrounds for this purpose.[5]

Many other adaptations of this "West Point" image of Lee were widely circulated in the North, but it was about August 1861 before these northern products were available for sale in Richmond.[6] The variations, including vignetted photographs (explained below), all show Lee with some sort of military uniform painted over the original civilian clothes. For many years it has been accepted by many collectors and dealers that this was an image of Lee in his Mexican War U.S. Army uniform, made about 1846!

Vignetted Photographs

A vignetted photograph is one in which the central image dissolves into the area around it, creating a soft blending of the image into the usually plain background. Vignettes of the Civil War period usually fade into a field of white. The effect was ordinarily achieved by printing the negative through a shaped (usually oval) opening in a piece of paper with translucent edges. It could also be accomplished by photographing the subject through a semi-transparent mask held close to the camera lens.

During the nineteenth century, oval vignetting was popular in portraiture. Because the technique could be used to copy some other photographer's work, it was also used to avoid registration and later copyright problems.

Because the special effect of vignetting was generally created by working with an existing negative or photograph rather than a sitting subject, no vignetted photograph of Lee can be considered an image made "from life," even when produced by the original photographer. In other words, if the same pose appears in a non-vignetted photographic format, then it stands to reason that all vignetted versions of that photograph must be alterations of the original version. One cannot "un-vignette" a photograph.

A vignetted version of the altered "West Point" photograph sold in the North by J. Gurney & Son of New York. Donald A. Hopkins

Vignetting is not to be confused with simply trimming (cropping) a photograph into an oval, circle, or some other shape and pasting it in the center of a card. Sometimes images thus trimmed and mounted were rephotographed to provide a standard-size rectangular negative showing the cropped photograph in the center of the field. Prints made from this new negative were then placed on a card mount in the usual fashion. An example of such a photograph is an extremely rare carte de visite of Lee produced by Sterling C. McIntyre, with a printed statement in tiny type around the image, "Photographed Richmond, 1861." It is also marked "copyright secured," which indicates that this particular presentation of the early Lee image originated with McIntyre. The image was marketed in France and the card had a French address on the bottom of the front and on the back.

This unique picture of a waist-up view, trimmed into an oval and then rephotographed, shows Lee with only stubble for a beard and a light-colored mustache. It is historically correct if it was produced in 1861, after Lee's ill-fated western Virginia campaign, at which time the General first decided to grow a beard.[7] This image is a very skillfully altered product based on the "West Point" daguerreotype

A version of the altered "West Point" photograph that was trimmed to oval shape, then re-photographed into carte de visite format by Sterling McIntyre of Richmond, Virginia, in 1861. Donald A. Hopkins

attributed to Brady, but unlike the other period alterations Lee's uniform coat is quite plain, with no epaulets or gold braid. This would be entirely compatible with Lee's rather spartan habits. One can speculate that McIntyre saw General Lee on the streets of Richmond in late 1861 and was inspired to produce this image. This particular altered presentation likely shows Lee as he looked in late 1861 much more accurately than any other of the many "doctored" images of the period.

Sterling C. McIntyre

Images by Sterling C. McIntyre are scarce, many having been made for the French or British markets. McIntyre had

trained as a dentist in France, and in 1844 advertised as a dentist as well as a "daguerrean" in Tallahassee, Florida. In 1845, he advertised colored daguerreotypes as he traveled around Florida. In 1847-1848 he worked in Charleston, South Carolina, for a short period before returning to Florida. In 1850, following a short interlude in New York, McIntyre moved west to San Francisco. He produced a widely acclaimed panoramic view of San Francisco for the Crystal Palace exhibition in London.[8] By 1851, after having sustained considerable loss in the San Francisco fire, he was in Nevada City, California, where he advertised as a photographer. He also practiced dentistry while becoming involved in a mining enterprise.[9] After a short time, he returned to the East. Little can be found out about him after that time, although there are wartime images from various studio locations in Florida.[10]

McIntyre's photographs often included a small Confederate flag as part of his props or his backmark. Judging by the appearance of some of his images of Confederate officers (i.e., General A. P. Hill), McIntyre sometimes resurrected an old technique previously employed by itinerant painters of children during the colonial days, that of using a standard child's body image, then painting only the faces. Similarly, in some cases McIntyre may have used a stock image of a torso in Confederate uniform to which he affixed a photograph of the head of the various officers to make his photographs. McIntyre's notation of "copyright secured" on his altered photograph of General Lee was quite unique in the early days of the Confederacy.

Copyrights and Photographs

In 1790, the United States passed its first copyright act, intended to protect books, maps, and charts. In 1802, prints were added to the protected works. Claims were to be recorded in the office of the clerks of district courts.[11] In 1861, the newly formed Confederacy adopted the existing U.S. copyright laws with the addition of protections for foreign authors whose states supplied reciprocal protection to citizens of the Confederacy, as well as a prohibition on importation of works from states which did not have reciprocal protection.[12]

It was not until March 3, 1865, shortly before the Civil War ended, that photographs became protected by copyright in the United States. The essential requirement was that the work be original. For example, if a photographer made an exact copy of another artist's work, he could not copyright his product because an exact copy does not constitute an original work. However, if a photographer enhanced or altered the original work, even slightly, he could then secure a copyright, but only on his modifications of the photograph. This regulation also required that a copy of each copyrighted work be deposited in the Library of Congress within a month of publication.

The image prepared by McIntyre in 1861 in Richmond could not be copyright-protected in the United States or the Confederacy as a photograph, although perhaps

the copyright did give him some protection in Europe, its intended market. His "copyright secured" likely referred to this carte de visite as a print, which he had prepared by dramatically altering a photograph of the original daguerreotype and then making a photographic negative of his work. Occasionally a photograph made before 1865 will bear a notation that it was "registered" in the District Clerk's office. By officially registering his photograph, a photographer could at least prove that he was the original artist of that particular image, even if he did not have copyright protection. Generally speaking, registration or copyright notations, if present at all, are found on the smaller sized images intended for the mass market.

An example of a carte de visite produced by E. & H. T. Anthony, New York, for both the Northern and Southern markets. Donald A. Hopkins

An important fact unknown to many modern collectors and dealers is that current copyright regulations prevent any photograph made before 1923 from being copyrighted. No photograph of Robert E. Lee, or any copy, alteration, or presentation of his image produced prior to 1923, has copyright protection. They are all in the public domain.[13]

Many other adaptations of the "West Point" daguerreotype were made showing Lee in uniform, often with a dark moustache and gold epaulets. This gold braid-fringed decoration on the shoulders of

Colonel Lee's dress uniform made a vivid impression on his youngest son.[14] There were even a few tintype copies made of this popular early wartime "doctored" image, laterally reversed as expected.

One widely circulated version was the vignetted chest view of the altered "West Point" image, published primarily for the northern market by Edward T. Anthony. Anthony's products are frequently found, not only in the North but in many old southern albums.

Edward Anthony

Edward Anthony was a civil engineer who later became interested in photography. He studied the daguerreotype technique under Samuel F. B. Morse before opening a gallery in 1842 in New York.[15] In 1847, he gave up the photography profession for a business selling photographic supplies, and by 1852 he was successful enough at his new venture to take in partners, including his brother Henry. They became the largest such firm operating in the United States during the Civil War period and immediately thereafter. In 1862, the firm's name was changed to E. & H. T. Anthony. By November 1863, they were advertising as manufacturers of photographic supplies, but also that they had for sale "over forty thousand different subjects," mostly in the way of copy portraits and stereographs.[16]

The Anthony brothers would obtain negatives from prominent photographers such as Mathew Brady, often in payment of bills for supplies, and publish photographs with their own "E. & H. T. Anthony" imprint on them, frequently with the indication that the picture was made from a Brady negative. By 1870, the company had expanded and was manufacturing cameras. In about 1875, when Brady was once again embroiled in his chronic financial prob-

lems, Anthony and Company acquired several thousand of his glass-plate negatives as payment on Brady's debt to the firm. Later, many of these Brady negatives, including many wartime images, were simply placed in storage.

In 1902, Anthony and Company merged with the Scovill and Adams Company to become Anthony and Scovill Company, later shortened to Ansco.

Unmarked and Pirated Photographs

A great many of the altered photographs of Robert E. Lee sold during the early years of the Civil War in both North and South are found with no indication of who made the photograph or who published it. It was easy enough to make a photograph of a photograph and then market this new,

A carte de visite of Robert E. Lee showing the "West Point" photograph as altered by Michael Miley of Lexington, Virginia, then hand-colored by Mrs. Lee. Donald A. Hopkins

A carte de visite of Mary Custis Lee made after the war by A. M. Hall of Alexandria, Virginia, hand-colored by Mrs. Lee. Donald A. Hopkins

An example of an altered "West Point" photograph with Mrs. Mary C. Lee's presentation in manuscript on the verso. Virginia Military Institute

"later-generation" image without a photographer's imprint. This omission of the artist's name and address was sometimes done simply to avoid registration and later copyright problems or, considering the prejudices of the day, in an effort to broaden the market to the North as well as the Confederacy. The new photographic copies were often slightly altered from the original by artistic enhancement or vignetting. These unmarked copies are today called "pirated" images. Pirating of a photograph was a frequent occurrence, especially when the subject was a famous or notorious person. However, many photographers simply did not mark their products, and on occasion the client, for reasons of his or her own, insisted that his photograph not be marked.

Michael Miley of Lexington, Virginia, not only copied the original "West Point" daguerreotype after the war; he produced altered copies of his own. Mrs. Mary Custis Lee hand-colored many of Miley's cartes de visite of her husband, along with pictures of herself. These little portraits, now eagerly sought by collectors, were used either for presentation to friends and family or to be sold to benefit the Robert E. Lee Memorial Church in Lexington. Many bear manuscript presentations on the reverse signed by Mrs. Lee. Mrs. Lee may have inadvertently contributed to the confusion regarding these altered photographs of her husband when, in her presentation on the back of the card, she sometimes wrote: "Gen. R. E. Lee when a Captain of Engineers in U. S. Army."[17]

Notes

Chapter 4: General Lee as He Never Was

[1] Inscription by Mary Custis Lee on the back of one of her artistically altered photographs of her husband, in author's collection; Robert E. Lee Memorial Church was formerly the Grace Episcopal Church located at the edge of the Washington College campus. General Lee attended services at this church.

[2] Eicher, *Robert E. Lee: A Life Portrait*, 42.

[3] William Turner, *Even More Confederate Faces* (Gaithersburg, MD, 1993), 16.

[4] "Sent to Fort Lafayette, from the *Baltimore Sun*, July 11, 1862," in *New York Times*, July 16, 1862. http://query.nytimes.com/gst/abstract.html; Fort Lafayette was used primarily to house political prisoners and Confederate officers. It was built on a natural island in the Narrows of New York Harbor.

[5] Editorial notice in *Photographic Times*, vol. 2, May 1872, 69; telephone interview with Lance Bendann, great-grandson of David Bendann, in 2006.

[6] Ruggles, *Photography in Virginia*, 49.

[7] Douglas Southall Freeman, *R. E. Lee: A Biography*, 4 vols. (New York, NY, 1934-1935), vol. 1, 577. In the Western Virginia Campaign in the fall of 1861 General Lee's poorly equipped troops were out-fought by the enemy, their defeat compounded by poor coordination among Lee's subordinate officers.

[8] Peter E. Palmquist, "Shadowcatching in El Dorado, 1849-1856," in Peter E. Palmquist, ed., *The Daguerreian Annual 1990; Official Yearbook of the Daguerreian Society* (Eureka, California, 1990), 177-178.; The Crystal Palace was a cast-iron and plate-glass building in London housing the Great Exhibition of 1851. Exhibitors from around the world gathered to display examples of their products. It was at the time the largest amount of glass ever seen in a building and did not require interior lights, thus a "Crystal Palace."

[9] Craig, "Sterling C. McIntyre," in *Craig's Daguerreian Registry*; During the San Francisco Fire of May, 1851, the business district virtually exploded in flames destroying three-fourths of the city.

[10] Palmquist, "Miscellaneous Daguerreian Biographies and Chronologies: Sterling C. McIntyre," in *The Daguerreian Annual 1990*, 190-193.

[11] U.S. Government Copyright Office, *United States Copyright Office: A Brief History*, (Washington, D.C., 2008), Circular 1a.

[12] Lionel Bently and Martin Kretschmer, eds., "Confederate States of America Copyright Act (1861)," *Primary Sources on Copyright* (1450-1900) (Cornell University Law Library, 2011). http://www.copyrighthistory.org/

[13] Peter Hirtle, *Copyright Term and the Public Domain in the United States*, Cornell University Copyright Information Center, Cornell University Library, 2011. http://copyright.cornell.edu/resources/publicdomain.cfm

[14] Lee, *Recollections and Letters*, 11.

[15] Samuel F. B. Morse (1791-1872) was a contributor to the invention of a telegraph system, a co-inventor of the Morse code, and an accomplished painter. In 1839 he became interested in photography and learned daguerreotypy well enough to teach others.

[16] "Something New," E. & H. T. Anthony Advertisement in *Harper's Weekly* (NY), November 7, 1863, 720.

[17] Elizabeth Brown Pryor, "Mary Anna Randolph Custis Lee (1807-1873)," in Brendan Wolfe, ed., *Encyclopedia Virginia*, Virginia Foundation for the Humanities, April 6, 2011. http://www.encyclopediavirginia.org/Lee_Mary_Anna_Randolph_Custis_1807-1873

A GENERAL STEPS FORWARD

"Lee wears his years well and strikes you as the incarnation of health and endurance." [1]

After mid-September 1862, following the Confederate Army's strategic withdrawal from Maryland after the battle of Sharpsburg (Antietam), General Lee instituted a series of morale-building grand reviews of his army.[2] A soldier described Lee's appearance at one such review: "His dress was inferior to that of his aides, being a simple cavalry uniform without insignia of rank." This observation quite well describes the General's appearance in two photographs and an engraving made several months later.[3]

"Booted and Spurred Lee"

The first photographs of General Lee in uniform taken during the war were made in 1863. Roy Meredith described a photograph of a full, standing Lee as his first formally posed photograph as a general and recorded that it was taken in the Richmond studio of Minnis and Cowell.[4] This was the so-called "Booted and Spurred" photograph. Meredith assigned no other poses to this photographic session. He was probably correct in that this was the first formally posed photograph of the General; the Minnis and Cowell embossed registration notation across the bottom of the card mount of many carte de visite versions of this portrait confirms that they indeed made the photograph in 1863. But there is room for skepticism regarding the location where the photograph was taken and under what circumstances.

In a blatant example of the "pirating" of a photograph, a well-known northern photographer and publisher, Charles D. Fredricks, photographically copied an original version of this classic photograph, including part of the Minnis and Cowell embossed registration imprint, across the bottom of the photograph before putting his own imprint on the back.

Charles DeForest Fredricks

C. D. Fredricks was working in a bank in New York City in 1843 when he began to study photography under Jeremiah Gur-

This "Booted and Spurred" photograph was taken by Minnis and Cowell of Richmond, Virginia, in early 1863. Virginia Historical Society

A Charles D. Fredricks of New York pirated copy of Minnis and Cowell's "Booted and Spurred" photograph of 1863. Donald A. Hopkins

ney. Later that same year, while on a business trip to Venezuela he began to make daguerreotypes of the area. He then began

extensive travels throughout South America as a photographer. In 1853, he opened a gallery in Paris, where he gained renown by

Minnis and Cowell's embossed stamp as found on their carte de visite versions of the "Booted and Spurred" photograph. Museum of the Confederacy

producing life-size photographs of subjects' heads, to be finished in pastels by painters. When he returned to New York he engaged in making high-quality paper photographs that he marked "Specialite." He opened a branch gallery in Havana, Cuba. Before his death in 1894, Fredricks became well known for large group photographs.[5]

The picture which was copied to make the pirated "Booted and Spurred" image must have been smuggled northward very soon after Minnis and Cowell produced the pose. The base for a head support—commonly used to keep a subject's head immobile—is clearly visible in this version. In most examples the negative has been altered to remove this from behind Lee's right foot. Indeed, any version of the "Booted and Spurred" image that does not show this head support base cannot be an original, unaltered, "from life" photograph. This is a good illustration of the principle that any photograph that does not contain all of the elements found in the original negative, excepting losses due to cropping or trimming, has been altered either in the negative or in the photograph itself.

The "Booted and Spurred" photograph was widely distributed as a woodcut engraving, including in both the *Illustrated London News* of June 4, 1864, and *Harper's Weekly* a month later.

The So-Called "In the Field" Photographs

A pair of photographs of Lee posed seated was also attributed to Minnis and Cowell by Roy Meredith. In one of these photographs Lee seems quite comfortable, with his uniform coat unbuttoned. Meredith opined that this particular photograph was "the first one taken after the war opened . . . the date was probably sometime in 1862."[6] In the second seated pose, Lee's heavy jacket is tightly buttoned up, and, due to similarities of the uniform, Meredith concluded that both were taken at the same photographic session. Also according to Meredith, these were possibly taken "in the field."

Lack of studio trappings and props could indeed lead Meredith and others to conclude that either of the two seated poses

An example of a print made from an original, unaltered negative of the "Booted and Spurred" photograph that still shows the head support base. Virginia Historical Society

An example of a print made from an altered negative that shows that the head support base has been removed. Southern Methodist University

An example of one of General Lee's "In the Field" photographs showing him seated with his coat unbuttoned. Southern Methodist University

may have been made in the field, even though studio portraits made in the South at the time often had plain backdrops and no props. The noted Civil War historian and author Richard B. Harwell flatly stated that General Lee had this buttoned-coat photograph made in late April 1863 at his headquarters near Fredericksburg by Minnis and Cowell, and nothing has been uncovered to refute that opinion.[7] However, both Meredith and Harwell may simply have been accepting at face value undocumented information found in an earlier (1912) work on Civil War photography.[8]

There are other intriguing possibilities. Consider for example that the "Booted and Spurred" portrait of Lee as well as both of the "In the Field" photographs could have been made at the same time. After all, as is the practice today, a photographer usually

made several exposures at the sitting of a subject, so as to get at least one satisfactory portrait. This was especially so when photographing prominent subjects.

A woodcut engraving showing General Lee, with field glasses in hand, leaning slightly on his sword, and wearing long cavalry boots with spurs, was based on a drawing done in the field in late 1862 or very early 1863 (shortly after the battle of Fredericksburg)[9] by British artist Frank Vizetelly. Vizetelly had been present during this campaign and remained around Lee's headquarters afterwards until he left by mid-January 1863 for Charleston. It is the only known drawing of Robert E. Lee done

An example of one of General Lee's "In the Field" photographs showing him with his coat buttoned. Museum of the Confederacy

from life. Vizetelly was a correspondent for the *Illustrated London News*, where this engraving first appeared on February 14, 1863, along with another engraving of Thomas J. ("Stonewall") Jackson.[10]

The important point to note here is that Vizetelly's drawing, made before mid-January 1863, proved that Lee had at hand at his field headquarters near Fredericksburg all the elements shown in Minnis and Cowell's Booted and Spurred photograph. He had field glasses, boots, spurs, broad-brimmed hat, and sword, as seen in both the woodcut and in Minnis and Cowell's photograph. In Vizetelly's drawing his coat is snugly buttoned up.

Many eyewitness descriptions of General Lee's uniforms worn during the war corroborate that of the Chaplain of the Army of Northern Virginia: "[He] was always simply attired and carefully avoided the gold lace and

THE CIVIL WAR IN AMERICA: GENERAL LEE, COMMANDER OF THE CONFEDERATE ARMY IN NORTHERN VIRGINIA.—FROM A SKETCH BY OUR SPECIAL ARTIST.

Woodcut engraving from drawing of Robert E. Lee made in the field in February 1863, by Frank Vizetelly of the *Illustrated London News*. Virginia Historical Society

feathers in which others delighted. During the war he usually wore a suit of gray, without ornament and no insignia of rank save the three stars on his collar which every Confederate colonel was entitled to wear. But he always kept a handsome though

equally simple uniform which he wore upon occasions of ceremony."[11] The thigh-length cavalry boots and the sword were likely part of his "simple uniform which he wore upon occasions of ceremony."

General Lee remained near Fredericksburg until the end of April 1863. Could the "Booted and Spurred" photograph have been taken at Lee's field headquarters? Except for the pattern in the floor cloth upon which the Booted and Spurred photograph was made, there is no hint of furniture, props, or decorative backdrops in any of the three photographs under consideration, except the head support base mentioned previously. In fact, careful examination of the backdrop near the floor in the "Booted and Spurred" image reveals that it is likely made of unevenly hung cloth or canvas. Floor cloths, basically heavy oilcloth decorated with simple patterns, were made to be placed over wooden, stone, or tamped earthen floors, and were the common floor coverings of the period.[12] Floor coverings were as easily portable as the canvas backdrops and adjustable head supports carried by traveling photographers.

Upper portion of the "Booted and Spurred" photograph compared to the "In the Field" photographs, showing similarity of Lee's uniform in each. Virginia Historical Society

of the coat, the lapels protrude out at an unattractive, odd angle, like butterfly wings, rather than lying flat against his chest as expected. Now consider the lapels in the image of Lee seated with the jacket unbuttoned. As noted by others over the years, the edges of the lapels are now trapped behind buttons to flatten them out against Lee's chest. This also looks somewhat unusual. Perhaps a third pose was made after tightly buttoning the coat, not only to shield against the inclement weather but to get rid of the pesky lapels altogether.

Conclusive evidence that at least two of these images, the "Booted and Spurred" pose and the "Buttoned Coat" pose, were made by Minnis and Cowell in 1863 lies in the embossed 1863 registration notation found on the bottom of some carte de visite versions of each of these images. This author

Examination of only the torso portion of the "Booted and Spurred" Lee alongside the two seated poses, with jacket unbuttoned and buttoned, leads to interesting observations. In all three pictures, the General apparently wears the same heavy uniform coat with a Confederate colonel's three stars rather than a general's wreathed insignia on the collar, and the stars are all of equal size.[13] However, his coat had two rows of eight buttons placed in pairs down the front in the manner of a general.[14] In the two photographs in which Lee's neck is visible, he seems to wear the same bulky, black bow tie. His hair and beard trim is identical in all three pictures. Note the position of the lapels of Lee's coat beginning with the "Booted and Spurred" pose. Probably because of the newness of the heavy material

"In the Field" pose with unbuttoned jacket compared to the "In the Field" photograph with buttoned coat (next page) and the "Booted and Spurred" photograph, showing similarity of Lee's uniform in each. Donald A. Hopkins

proposes consideration of an alternate theory: that all three images were made at the same photographic session and in the field, the last two after the General had unslung his binoculars, removed his sword belt, and had taken a seat.

"In the Field" pose with buttoned jacket compared to the "In the Field" photograph with unbuttoned coat (previous page) and the "Booted and Spurred" photograph, (previous page) showing similarity of Lee's uniform in each. Alabama Department of Archives and History

If these three photographs were indeed made in the field, when were they made? Evidence suggests that they were produced after the Fredericksburg campaign ended in December 1862 but prior to the May 1863 battle of Chancellorsville.[15]

A Robert E. Lee/Stonewall Jackson Connection?

On March 30, 1863, General Lee became acutely ill with respiratory/cardiac problems, requiring medical care at the home of Thomas Yerby, an estate called Belvoir located a few miles from Fredericksburg. Lee was ensconced in the upstairs of the house for several days while he recovered, after which he returned to his headquarters 1½ miles away. The heavy uniform Lee wears in the two poses which Meredith considered "In the Field" photographs correlates well with a statement in a letter from Lee to his wife that the weather in early April 1863 was "worse than any time during the winter."[16] On April 20, Stonewall Jackson brought his wife and baby daughter to Belvoir, where they occupied the same quarters previously used by General Lee. Lee remained a frequent visitor to Belvoir during the remainder of April.[17]

During the last part of April, General Jackson had a photograph made at Belvoir by a Richmond photographer. A member of Jackson's staff, Henry Kyd Douglas, recorded:[18]

"Having been warned that he could not hope to get General Jackson to sit for his picture, he (the photographer) resorted to strategy. He called upon the General and informed him that he had been sent from Richmond to get General Lee's photograph in camp, but that General Lee had surprised him by declining unless General Jackson would have his taken first. General Jackson hesitated and then, saying that General Lee ought to have his picture taken for the people and should not get out of it that way, he consented and Minnis got his photograph."[19]

This begs the question: "Did General Lee have his photograph taken by this same photographer around the same time also?"

Another account, entirely compatible with Douglas' version, appears in a detailed biography of General Jackson which relates that the photographer appeared at the house one day and that "Mrs. Jackson persuaded her husband to sit for a photograph." The photograph was taken in the "main hall" of the house where the wind through the front-to-back passageway created such a draft that it caused Jackson to show a frown in the resulting image.[20] One can easily see that Jackson's uniform coat is just as tightly buttoned up as Lee's in one of the "In the Field" photographs.

Additional information about this photographic encounter at least makes clear who actually took Jackson's photograph. In July 1863, the *Southern Illustrated News* answered skeptics who doubted the authenticity of the Jackson photograph as follows: "The newspaper wished to announce that the picture was taken for us by Mr. D. T. Cowell of the Minnis Gallery. Through the kindness of a friend we were enabled to procure for Mr. Cowell a letter of introduction to Gen. Jackson, who immediately upon the arrival of the artist at his headquarters at Fredericksburg, consented to sit for the picture. . . ."[21]

Since it is a fact that General Jackson had his photograph made by Cowell at this time, it is certainly reasonable to assume that Lee sat for photographs in the field at about the same time. Whatever the actual circumstances, when Cowell gathered his supplies, chemicals, and equipment for a foray into the field during harsh weather, one would expect him to make the effort as productive as possible by obtaining as many marketable photographs as possible, especially one of General Lee.

Additional evidence that Stonewall Jackson's photograph was made in 1863 is found in

Minnis and Cowell's embossed registration stamp commonly found near the bottom of their carte de visite versions of these pictures. This is the same stamp mentioned in conjunction with the "Booted and Spurred" and Buttoned Coat photographs of Lee. Furthermore, these small images of both Lee and Jackson that bear this embossed registration note are often found mounted on similar plain, unadorned cards. The earliest presentation of the Unbuttoned Coat photograph as a carte de visite examined by the author is rather crude by later standards, reflecting the scarcity of photographic supplies in the Confederacy. The card mount is of very thin, rather brittle cardboard. The albumen silver image itself is mounted on thick paper, hand-trimmed into a near oval shape, and then glued into the center of the card. Its redeeming attribute is the extreme sharpness and clarity of the unenhanced photograph itself, suggesting that it is a very early printing, possibly from the original negative, though it has no imprint.

Registration notations such as those used by Minnis were commonly placed on pictures of famous or notorious figures intended for the broad market, usually in the relatively inexpensive carte de visite format. Perhaps the Unbuttoned Coat image was not originally intended for such wide distribution. After all, according to Richmond newspapers of mid-1863, Virginia-made cartes de visite of Southern notables were still quite a novelty and were not widely available.[22]

Until very recently, Minnis and Cowell's registration imprints have not been found on the pose of Lee in his unbuttoned coat, and indeed a few students of Lee photographs have expressed doubt that it was produced by Minnis and Cowell. Some have attributed it to the Bendann brothers of Baltimore, but this scenario was rejected out of hand by Meredith.[23] Copies of this image are occasionally seen with the Bendann imprint, but it seems unlikely that either of the brothers would have attempted to go through the Union lines in 1863 to make a photograph, which would have jeopardized their successful business in federally occupied Baltimore. After all, they were already suspected of being Confederate sympathizers.

The uncertainties about who made the original photograph of General Lee seated with unbuttoned jacket, and in what year it was made, can now be laid to rest. A catalog illustration of a carte de visite-size, small, oval, salt print copy of this picture was located in the archives of a well-known auction house. The original photograph, which bore a Minnis and Cowell 1863 registration imprint, was sold long ago, and only the low-resolution illustration reproduced from the auction catalog is available for examination. However, the registration notation across the bottom is clearly

visible.[24] Rather than having an embossed notation of registration, as did Minnis and Cowell's other photographs of Lee and of Jackson, this one has a printed registration note across the bottom. The note on the bottom of this rare carte de visite reads, "Entered according to Act of Congress in the year 1863, by Minnis & Cowell in the Clerk's Office of the District Court of the Confederate States for the Eastern District of Virginia."

Additional confirmation that Minnis and Cowell produced this photograph in 1863 lies in the recent discovery of a period photograph which carries their embossed registration across the bottom. This particular, slightly elongated carte de visite is imprinted on the back "Premier Photographic Gallery, R. Wearn, Artist, Columbia, South Carolina," along with the frequently seen statement that "Negative kept, duplicates can be had."[25] This rare photograph was purchased several years ago at an estate sale in Rock Hill, South Carolina, and has been in a private collection since that time.

ered according to Act of Congress, in the year 1863, by MINNIS & COWELL, in the Clerk's Office of the District Court of the Confederate States for the Eastern District of Virginia.

A salt print in small carte de visite format of the unbuttoned coat pose of the "In the Field" photographs bears a printed Minnis and Cowell registration notation that it was registered in 1863. Swann Auction Galleries

Extremely rare, possibly unique, copy of Minnis and Cowell's "In the Field" unbuttoned coat image bearing their embossed 1863 registration stamp along with a backmark of R. Wearn, Columbia, South Carolina. Donald A. Hopkins

It is identical to a photograph held by the Museum of the Confederacy, except on the latter there is no Minnis and Cowell imprint, just that of R. Wearn as a backmark. This unusual combination of an uncropped, rectangular-shaped version of this picture, on a card with Minnis and Cowell's embossed registration stamp yet bearing a South Carolina photographer's imprint on the verso, is somewhat of an enigma. It is also extremely rare; the photograph illustrated here is the only one known which shares these traits.[26]

Some have speculated that Wearn either obtained a supply of cards already embossed by Minnis and Cowell, or had Minnis place his embossed stamp on the South Carolinian's imprinted card(s) before mounting his photographs on the card support. This begs the question, why would Wearn go to this trouble? After all, Wearn could have done like other photographers of the day and copied this photograph with impunity. The registration stamp gave no copyright protection whatsoever to Minnis and Cowell because at the time photographs were not copyright-pro-tected. This embossed stamp only certified who made the original photograph and in what year.

Examination of the back of the card reveals two certain facts. Wearn's imprint was mechanically printed on the card as opposed to being hand-stamped. Also, the slightly elevated strip along the bottom of the card is the result of the pressure of Minnis and Cowell's embossing stamp across the bottom of the front of the card. This strongly suggests that Richard Wearn supplied the card(s) bearing his printed imprint to Minnis and Cowell, who then embossed it with their registration stamp when they mounted the paper photograph on the card. Once

Backmark of R. Wearn, Columbia, South Carolina, on Minnis and Cowell photograph. Donald A. Hopkins

Wearn purchased his initial photograph(s) from Minnis and Cowell, he could rephoto-graph it, leaving off Minnis and Cowell's registration stamp, and make a negative from which he could produce a number of copy prints exactly like the one in the Museum of the Confederacy. A simple gentlemen's agreement between artists would have allowed this unorthodox transaction. It is certainly possible that the well-worn copy illustrated here was actually Wearn's original copy from which he made his negatives. There is no way to know.

Richard Wearn

Richard Wearn, born on the Isle of Man, came to North Carolina as a child and later became a South Carolina artist. He was recorded as a daguerreian in Anderson in 1854, in partnership with someone named Richardson. They obtained many of their supplies from George S. Cook of Charleston. By 1856, Wearn was advertising a traveling daguerreotype and ambrotype gallery in Abbeville, but by 1858 he was partners with C. H. Kingsmore in Newberry. He opened a gallery in Columbia in 1859, operating it with William P. Hix until Wearn's death in 1874, by suicide.[27]

The photograph of Lee with his lapels trapped under the upper buttons of his unbuttoned coat proved to be a masterpiece. It became one of the best-known photographs of the General and was reproduced during and after the war as copies of the original photograph, altered copies of the original, etchings, engravings, paintings, lithographs, and all sorts of photomechanical reproductions.

Many versions of these Minnis and Cowell 1863 photographs were copied as cartes de visite by Northern photographers and publishers for sale in their market. They were sold in Canada and even sent through the Federal naval blockade for sale in Europe.

Blockade-Run Photographs

The Federal naval blockade of Southern ports, although instituted immediately after the opening of hostilities, was not very effective initially. Southern blockade runners became the lifeline linking the Confederacy with Europe. As the war progressed, however, an increasing percentage of ships attempting to enter or leave Confederate ports was captured or sunk.

Not only were materials of war imported, but many necessities and even luxuries were also delivered to Southern ports. Exports from the South were primarily cotton and to-

bacco, but among them also were photographic images or negatives for the European market. Enterprising European photographers/publishers even returned some of these images mounted on cards imprinted with their logo back to Confederate ports. Many "blockade-run" images have been found in old Southern photographic albums.

George W. Minnis and Daniel T. Cowell

From 1847 until 1860, George W. Minnis had a daguerreotype gallery in Petersburg, Virginia, having studied the art in

An example of a "blockade-run" carte de visite bearing a Confederate flag logo on its verso, which was sold by C. B. Walker in London and published by S. C. McIntyre of Pensacola, Florida. Donald A. Hopkins

Philadelphia under Marcus Root. In 1852, he had branched out to Richmond, where he was located at 35 Main Street, "Upstairs," in partnership with John W. Watson. Watson was the principal operator. Minnis also employed Alexander Bagley that same year. By 1853, Minnis was preparing a new gallery at 146 Main Street, Richmond. He also operated a branch of his business in Lynchburg, Virginia. In about 1857, the entrepreneurial Minnis also operated the "Photographic and Pearl-type Gallery" at 47 Sycamore Street, Petersburg. In 1859, he was listed at 13 Sycamore Street, and boarded at "Mrs. Wright's." At the same time his gallery in Richmond was now at 197 Main Street, and he was reportedly one of the most prosperous photographers south of New York.

Minnis hired Daniel T. Cowell as a photographer in 1860, now listing his gallery's address as 215 Main Street, Richmond, C. R. Rees' old address. Cowell was quite talented in the collodion/albumen techniques of photography.[28] In 1860, Minnis and associates won the top prize in a photographic competition in Richmond.[29] In March 1863, their gallery advertised carte de visite photographs of General A. P. Hill, among others. This was newsworthy enough to be mentioned by the *Southern Illustrated News* in June 1863.[30]

In April 1864, Minnis advertised that his gallery would be closed for an undetermined time. Apparently, Cowell left for Petersburg at that time. On April 15, 1865, after Federal troops occupied Richmond, the *Richmond Whig* reported that Minnis' gallery, which had now reopened, suffered damage from fire.[31]

By mid-July 1865, George Minnis was preparing to move into a new, L-shaped building fronting on both Main and 9th Streets.[32] His second-story studio was listed in the Richmond City Directory of 1866 at 6 North 9th Street. For a short time after September 1866, he worked with Julian Vannerson. Within less than a year, Minnis moved from Richmond to Petersburg, at which time he may well have sold his wartime negatives to Vannerson.

It is important to note that, at that time, Vannerson and Minnis between them possessed the only original "from life" negatives[33] of Robert E. Lee, with the possible exception of the photograph of Lee and his horse taken at Petersburg near the end of the war. Many of these negatives later came into the possession of George Cook, and can today be found at the Valentine Richmond History Center in Richmond, Virginia.

In Petersburg Minnis worked as a photographer for the Rockwell Gallery, which had been in operation during the war. James R. Rockwell had earlier formed an association with Daniel T. Cowell, the same artist who had worked with Minnis in Richmond. By 1873, Minnis was in business with Edwin J. Rees in Petersburg.

Daniel T. Cowell was first noted as a daguerreotypist in 1851-1852 in New Haven, Connecticut. At some point prior to 1856, he became head operator in the gallery of J. H. Whitehurst in Baltimore, Maryland. From 1856 until an undetermined date, P. L. Perkins employed Cowell at his gallery at 99 Baltimore Street, Baltimore. By 1859, Cowell was listed as a daguerreotypist in Richmond, Virginia, without a business address; but in 1860 he was listed as working for G. W. Minnis at 217 Main Street, Richmond.[34] The business always remained in the name of Minnis, though credits on some cartes de visite included Cowell.

Shortly after the war, Cowell was working in Petersburg, where he collaborated with J. R. Rockwell in producing the so-called "Military Medallion." It is interesting to note that the central photograph in this collage is General Lee represented by a variation of the "In the Field" photograph, the original of which was evidently made in 1863 by Cowell. Cowell returned to New Haven sometime later, and in 1869 was listed there.

Determining the Size of the Original Negative

This classic image illustrates one of the many puzzles a serious student of old photographs faces. What was the size of the original "from life" negative? Was it a whole-plate glass image? Or something smaller, or possibly larger?

A fragile, soiled, and faded example of one of the 1863 Minnis and Cowell images was found in its original 1860s-period oval frame. The photographer's imprint, if it ever existed, had been trimmed away long ago. In this case it appears that a second-generation wet-plate negative was made from a print of the original photograph which had been greatly "enhanced" and then photographed. The new negative was used to print pictures such as this one, which show detail of beard, hair, and even the fabric of Lee's suit. The new albumen/silver prints were then trimmed to

An example of a large-format colloid/albumen print, 6 inches x 8 inches, of Robert E. Lee, taken in 1863, later enhanced and re-photographed, then cropped to an oval shape. Donald A. Hopkins

an oval shape. Was this perhaps the size of the negative made at the original sitting, i.e., whole-plate, or is it a photographic enlargement of the original? One can only speculate.

It was easy enough to photographically copy images onto a larger or smaller glass plate and then have a new, later-generation negative of a size different than the original. Thus a photograph, even with the imprint of the original photographer, could have been printed from one of these later-generation negatives, and even though marketed today as an original, "from life" image may not be so. Unfortunately, securing valid documentation of which size plate the photographer originally used may be difficult or even impossible. Occasionally a photographer or publisher would place a statement on the photograph that it was made from the original negative. Also, in theory at least, after March 1865, the Library of Congress should have prints from all original negatives for which a photographer sought to secure copyright protection. Later on a fine was imposed for non-compliance with this regulation. Any such photographic prints in the Library of Congress positively identified as part of a copyright registration would identify with certainty the size of the original glass-plate negative.

One would expect that the clearest and sharpest image would be the original, and indeed these factors are usually considered in attempts to deter-mine the size of the original negative plate. An ex-tremely clear and sharp (although somewhat dam-aged) "cabinet card"[35] was pro-duced by George S. Cook after 1880, perhaps from an original Minnis and Cow-ell 1863 negative. Even though it is slightly faded and stained, one can still make out great detail of Lee's collar insignia and much of the design on his uniform buttons. This cabinet card suggests that the negative Cook started with to make this print was of whole-plate size.

When this image is compared with the original pose, which showed more of Lee's lower torso as well as background lateral to each of his arms, one can see that this image is cropped from the bottom and the sides, removing about one-third of the original image in both length and width to fit the cabinet card. Therefore the original image may have been about one-third larger than this cabinet card version, i.e., whole-plate

An example of a cabinet card-size photograph of Robert E. Lee printed by George S. Cook of Rich-mond, Virginia, in about 1880. Donald A. Hopkins

size. Because of this photograph's clarity, this author believes that Cook began with a whole-plate negative (possibly the original "from life" plate), used vignetting tech-niques and otherwise enhanced it, then cropped it to cabinet-card size to produce this version. Minnis' original negatives and prints can be traced from his studio, through Julian Vannerson with whom he partnered briefly after the war, then on to the Davies family when Vannerson sold out. In about 1891, Davies sold his negatives to George S. Cook.

George S. Cook

Twenty-year-old George S. Cook (1819-1902) was studying painting in New Orleans in 1839 when photography was introduced in America. He immediately espoused the new medium and helped spread photography throughout the South until 1849. First he ran a gallery in New Orleans before setting out to teach the trade to others in small towns. He would teach a few students in each town while establishing a studio, then sell the business to a promising student. He settled in Charleston, South Carolina, before the Civil War.

During the war, Cook was one of the foremost Confederate photographers and earned fame by recording the adverse effects of the war on Charleston and Fort Sumter. He further satisfied his entrepreneurial instincts by participating in blockade running during the war, selling photographic materials and supplies by mail order, and even marketing a patent medicine called "Charleston Water."

In April 1880, Cook's older son, George LaGrange Cook, took over the studio in Charleston while his father branched out to Richmond.[36] Cook bought the business of D. H. Anderson at 1311 Main Street, including some 20,000 negatives. He also bought out other Richmond photographers who were retiring or moving. In about 1891, he purchased the business of the Lee

Gallery from John W. Davies and family. Davies had acquired the negatives from the Vannerson and Jones Studio about 1869, which had in turn obtained at least some of George Minnis' negatives.

By this means Cook amassed the most complete collection of original wartime photographs of Robert E. Lee available. It is certainly possible that Cook even obtained negatives from Charles Rees when he left for Petersburg. According to a report in the *Daily Dispatch* in May 1935, Cook aggregated 12 different wartime negatives of Robert E. Lee among his acquisitions. This is a very revealing statement that strongly suggests that Cook might have acquired every existing "from life" negative (or a wartime copy of this negative) made as Lee sat for photographs during the conflict. It would include three negatives made by Minnis and Cowell, four made by Vannerson, three erroneously attributed to John Davies, and one by an unknown photographer at Petersburg. The twelfth negative might have been a version of the early, war-doctored "West Point" photograph, or perhaps a duplicate negative. When E. V. Valentine examined this group of Cook's negatives and prints, he declared the three-quarter-length torso view made by Vannerson to be the best likeness.[37]

George Cook remained an active photographer all his life. During the 1880s, his younger son, Huestis, became interested in photography and eventually went into business with his father. After George Cook's death in 1902, Huestis operated the Richmond studio until 1946, when he retired. In 1954, the Valentine Richmond History Center acquired the George S. Cook Collection from Mary Latimer Cook, Huestis Cook's widow.

Notes

Chapter 5: A General Steps Forward

[1] British artist Frank Vizetelly reporting on Lee's appearance in the field in late 1862. Douglas W. Bostick, *The Confederacy's Secret Weapon: The Civil War Illustrations of Frank Vizetelly* (Charleston, SC, 2009), 95.

[2] The Sharpsburg (Antietam) Campaign was the Confederates' first attempt to invade the North. It resulted in the bloodiest single day of the entire war before Lee, facing a battered and largely stationary Federal force began a strategic withdrawal from Maryland back to Virginia.

[3] Smith, "As They Saw General Lee," *Civil War Times Illustrated*, October 1986, 21.

[4] Meredith, *The Face of Robert E. Lee*, 37.

[5] Craig, "Charles D. Fredricks," in Craig's *Daguerreian Registry*.

[6] Meredith, *The Face of Robert E. Lee*, 30-35.

[7] Richard Harwell, illustrated typescript note, n.d., museum collection, Virginia Historical Society, Richmond, Virginia. Copy in author's collection.

[8] Trent, *"Robert E. Lee,"* vol. 10, 55.

[9] The battle of Fredericksburg on December 13, 1862 resulted in a crushing defeat of the Federals who fell back across the Rappahannock River after suffering nearly three times the number of casualties as the Confederates who fought from behind nearly impregnable lines.

[10] Bostick, *The Confederacy's Secret Weapon*, 95-96.

[11] John William Jones, *Personal Reminiscences, Anecdotes, and Letters: Gen. Robert E. Lee* (New York, NY, 1875), 146.

[12] Linoleum was not invented until the mid-1860s. Ralph Parsons, "Linoleum: A Chiswick Invention," *Brentford Chiswick Local History Journal*, Journal 5, 1996. http://brentfordandchiswicklhs.org.uk/local-history/industries-and-crafts/linoleum-a-chiswick-invention/

[13] A uniform jacket worn in later photographs had a larger star as the center insignia.

[14] Philip Katcher, *American Civil War Armies (3): Staff, Specialist and Maritime Services* (London: 1988), 21.

[15] The Chancellorsville campaign, fought during the first four days of May 1862, resulted in Lee's outnumbered troops out-maneuvering and out-fighting the Federals before sending them in retreat. Stonewall Jackson was fatally injured by friendly fire during the campaign.

[16] Freeman, *Lee*, vol. 2, 501-502.

[17] Freeman, *Lee*, vol. 2, 506. Lenoir Chambers, *Stonewall Jackson* (Wilmington, NC, 1988), vol. 2, 357.

[18] Henry Kyd Douglas was known to exaggerate and embellish his narratives, and became quite eccentric in his old age.

[19] Henry Kyd Douglas, *I Rode with Stonewall* (Chapel Hill, NC, 1940), 200.

[20] Chambers, *Stonewall Jackson*, vol. 2, 360. Mary Anna Jackson, *Memoirs of Stonewall Jackson* (Louisville, KY, 1895), 409-410.

[21] Neely, Holzer, and Boritt, *Confederate Image*, 112.

[22] Ruggles, *Photography in Virginia*, 49.

[23] Meredith, *The Face of Robert E. Lee*, 30.

[24] Swann Galleries, "Portrait of Robert E. Lee; Salt Print, Mtd." catalog entry in *Important 19th and 20th Century Photographs*, New York, NY, October 11, 2000, Lot 7.

[25] Telephone interview with Bryan Davis, owner, *Charleston Underground Civil War Relics*, February 3, 2012. Telephone interview with Dr. Edward West, collector and prior owner of the photograph, March 19, 2012.

[26] The Minnis and Cowell embossed registration stamp on the "unbuttoned coat" photograph remains extremely rare though an additional one on a CDV in the collection of Dr. John O'Brien has been brought to the attention of the author.

[27] Craig, "Richard Wearn," in *Craig's Daguerreian Registry*. Harvey S. Teal, *Partners with the Sun: South Carolina Photographers*, 1840-1940 (Columbia, SC, 2001), 70-71.

[28] Craig, "George W. Minnis," in *Craig's Daguerreian Registry*.

[29] "List of Premiums Awarded at the Seventh Annual exhibition of the Virginia Mechanic's Institute, which Closed on the Night of the 31st Oct., 1860," *Richmond Daily Dispatch*, Nov. 1, 1860. http://dlxs.richmond.edu/d/ddr/

[30] Ruggles, *Photography in Virginia*, 49.

[31] Gorman, "Civil War Richmond" (Richmond, VA, 2008). http://www.mdgorman.com/Written_Accounts/newspaper

[32] "Building in the Burnt District of Richmond," *The Norfolk Post*, July 13, 1865. http://chroniclingamerica.com/

[33] Discussed in detail in Chapter 7.

[34] Craig, "Daniel T. Cowell," in *Craig's Daguerreian Registry*.

[35] This format is explained in more detail in the next chapter.

[36] Jack C. Ramsay, Jr., *Photographer...Under Fire: The Story of George S. Cook*, 1819-1902 (Green Bay, WI, 1994), 101-102.

[37] Untitled newspaper clipping, *Richmond Times Dispatch*, May 17, 1935. *George S. and H. Cook Papers*, 1912-1925, 1929, Manuscript Collection No. 28, Valentine Richmond History Center, Richmond, Virginia.

CHAPTER 6

IN ALL HIS MARTIAL SPLENDOR

"General Lee is, almost without exception,
the handsomest man of his age I ever saw."[1]

In the spring of 1864, while in Richmond, Lee agreed to have a series of portraits made for the use of a Virginia artist studying in Berlin. Edward V. Valentine was to sculpt a small statue of Lee for sale at a benefit to be held in Liverpool, England, for Confederate prisoners' relief. The project was enthusiastically promoted by a group of Richmond ladies, who gave the General some high, white shirt collars to wear for the photographic sitting at Julian Vannerson's gallery.[2] Collectively, this group of portraits is known as Lee's "Blockade Images," as they were sent to Valentine in Europe through the Federal naval blockade. After receiving these photographs on May 5, having never seen General Lee in person, Valentine began work on May 13, 1864. The statuette was cast in Europe on October 17 and photographed there on November 9, 1864.[3] (Appendix C)

For many years the general belief was that photographer Vannerson made only one standing pose at this sitting. In 1983, an additional pose was recognized, a full standing pose, with Lee's sword at more of an angle from his side and other subtle differences.[4] That image, for purposes of convenience, is called "Standing Pose 2." The example shown on the following page, though heavily foxed and stained, is displayed in its large-format original state. Because this "Standing Pose 2" is slightly out of focus, some have speculated that after printing only a very few of the original whole-plate images the plate was broken or discarded. There is no clear evidence that a copy of this particular photograph was sent to Valentine in Europe. The Museum of the Confederacy in Richmond has a copy of this image produced by Huestis C. Cook of Richmond in the late 1800s or early 1900s. Whether this was made from the original negative or is a copy print is unclear. Only a very few examples of "Standing Pose 2" are known to exist. An example of the more common "Standing Pose 1" is whole-plate size and was likely printed from the original negative, as the negative had not yet been altered to remove the evidence of the head support base seen behind the General's right heel. This head support base can be seen to better advantage between his feet in "Standing Pose 2." Postwar copies of "Standing Pose 1" were often enhanced or altered by obscuring

This is a copy of a standing pose, for many years thought to be the only such pose made by Julian Vannerson of Richmond in early 1864 for Edward V. Valentine to be sent through the blockade to Europe. Stratford Hall

This is a copy of a standing pose, unrecognized for many years, made by Julian Vannerson of Richmond in early 1864 for Edward V. Valentine to be sent through the blockade to Europe. Donald A. Hopkins

evidence of the head support base and even decorating what had originally been a very plain backdrop.

A left profile and a near frontal view facing slightly to the right completed this series of Vannerson photographs of Lee. The sharp left profile photograph, as shown in Meredith's compilation of Lee photographs, reveals that the original negative was a three-quarter view showing the General seated in a chair in front of a plain background. The chair in which Lee sits rigidly upright to expose his upper body in left profile view is not the usual fancy posing chair found in photographers' studios of the period. Instead, it is a common side chair with no arms to obstruct

the camera's view. The original photograph, complete with chair, was useful as a model for a statue, but was most likely not considered to be an attractive photograph for the market. An exhaustive search has not located a print made from the original negative; a high-resolution scan of an original halftone picture is all that is available for presentation in this study.[5] This particular portrait is most often represented by only a vignetted head, neck, and upper torso view of Lee, a much more marketable variation of this pose. It is doubtful that more than a few prints were made from the original negative before it was laid aside in favor of its vignetted version, which removed the chair from the image.

An example of a postwar copy of the Vannerson "Standing Pose 1" that was produced as a CDV by Lumpkin and Tomlinson of Richmond, Virginia, after alteration and enhancement, showing removal of the head support clamp base and embellishment of the backdrop. Howard McManus

A right oblique near frontal view from this sitting with Vannerson has become one of the better known photographs of the General. Both sitting poses were reproduced well into the postwar period as cartes de visite and cabinet cards.

Julian Vannerson

Julian Vannerson, a native of Virginia, returned to Richmond in about 1860 from Washington, D.C., where he had been working for James E. McClees. McClees was quite prominent as a photographer, and in fact some students of the subject think

A copy of a later half-tone print showing General Lee seated, made from a print of the original Vannerson left profile made in Richmond, Virginia, in early 1864. Donald A. Hopkins

An example of the much more common left profile presentation of Julian Vannerson's photograph made in early 1864 in Richmond, Virginia. Library of Congress

he prepared the first collodion negatives in the United States. While in Washington, Vannerson was credited with several famous photographs of a delegation of Sioux Indians.[6] After his arrival in Richmond, he was associated with John Thomas Smith for a short while at the old Whitehurst gallery location at 77 Main Street in Richmond. By the time the war started, Smith was no longer associated with the gallery. In February 1862, Vannerson's studio was damaged by fire, but he was back in business at the same location at least by the end of July of the same year.[7] His wartime cartes de visite are marked simply "Vannerson, Photographic Artist, 77 Main St., Richmond, Virginia," often on plain, unembellished cards. Richmond sales tax records for 1863 indicate that Vannerson was the only photographer operating in the city in August 1863 when this tax data was recorded. For a brief period in April and May 1864, he worked under contract for the Confederate government.[8] Later records show him as purchasing business licenses up until February 1865, which would have allowed him to work until 1866. In May 1865, he was at the same 77 Main Street location, now in

An example of the near frontal view of General Lee made in early 1864 by Julian Vannerson of Richmond, Virginia, and sent through the federal naval blockade to Edward V. Valentine in Europe to use as a model for his statuette. Library of Congress

association with C. E. Jones. The sales tax registry for 1865 listed his address as "Main between 14th and 15th Street."[9]

In July 1865, as the "burnt district" of Richmond was being rebuilt, a building was under construction at the site of P. H. Taylor's old stand on Main Street near 10th Street for John W. Davies & Son's book and music store.[10] The second floor was to be occupied by "Vannerson & Co."[11] In November 1865, Davies' "Richmond Music Exchange" reopened. This would be the earliest that a Vannerson and Jones backmark would have carried the same address as Davies' music store, which was 188 Main Street.

By early 1866, Vannerson and Jones were firmly re-established in business, at which time they sent copy negatives and prints of the Lees' "family portraits," including photographs of the General, to a publisher in Canada for use in a book.[12] In April 1866, the partners were still operating out of two locations in Richmond, 77 and 188 Main Street (upstairs). Dates of cancellation of revenue stamps on their cartes de visite imprinted with only the 188 Main Street address indicate that by May 1866 they had consolidated their operations in Richmond to their gallery over the music store. Only

Vannerson and Jones photographs made between November 1865 and May 1866 show two street addresses in Richmond.

The following excerpt from a letter confirms that in April 1866 General Lee was accumulating images from Vannerson for personal use and dispersal:

Richmond 13th April 1866
Genl R. E. Lee
Dear Genl,

….All are well & I have no news – On the other side is statement of balance of acct showing in your favor of $111.98 which I will dispose of as you direct – Vannerson would not accept pay for the 2 doz. photographs. With kindest regards from all to all I am, yours faithfully.

James K. Caskie[13]

Richmond's street numbering system changed early in 1866, redesignating Vannerson's old street address as well as the address for the Music Exchange. An 1866 business directory gives Vannerson's address as 1427 Main Street, which is apparently the same location between 14th and 15th Streets previously known as 77 Main Street. There are also photographs of this period bearing Vannerson and Jones imprints with a 920 Main Street address, which seems to have been the new designation of the 188 Main Street location above the Davies Music Exchange.

Any Robert E. Lee image with a Vannerson & Jones imprint, whatever the street address, should be considered a postwar product of 1865-66. About September 1866, Vannerson's connection with Jones was terminated, and shortly thereafter Vannerson had a brief association with G. W. Minnis. This was followed by another short-lived relationship with a photographer named Levy.[14] Their backmark on

cartes de visite, which reads "Vannerson & Levy, Photographers, No. 737 Main Street (Two doors above Spotswood Hotel) Richmond, Va." appears on a photograph signed and presented on September 1, 1867, by General Lee and his wife. Little is known about Levy, but he might have been a member of an old and prominent Jewish family of Richmond. At a recent auction a salt print of Libby Prison in Richmond, supposedly made in 1863, was attributed to "C. Levy" of Richmond, but whether or not he was the same man later associated with Vannerson is not clear.[15] After September 1867, Vannerson operated as Vannerson & Co. He remained actively engaged as a photographer in Richmond for probably no more than two years. He was not listed in the Richmond Business Directory for 1869, evidently having departed the city. In 1869, he sold his business, including his extensive archive of negatives, to the Davies family, who established and advertised "The Lee Gallery – successor to Vannerson & Jones."[16] Apparently Vannerson relocated to Norfolk. In 1875, he was working with D. H. Anderson in Norfolk and in Richmond.

Edward V. Valentine and the Vannerson Photographs

Edward Virginius Valentine (1838-1930) was an American sculptor who was born in Richmond, Virginia, and studied in Europe. Over the years he produced numerous busts and statues of Confederate heroes. Valentine sculpted a bust of Lee shortly before the old General's death and later made the recumbent statue for Robert E. Lee's tomb in Lexington, Virginia. Among his more famous works is his bronze statue of Lee that resides in the National Statuary Hall collection in the United States Capitol building.

Three of Valentine's personal photographs of Lee were recently sold at auction. These

Modelled in Berlin before seeing general Lee. The Statuette which was sold for the Souttern Cause — at the Souttern Bazaar in Liverpool England Con May 9, 1864 Contr Oct 17, 1864

A photograph, found among the papers of Edward V. Valentine, of his statuette, which he made in Europe in early 1864 based on photographs made by Julian Vannerson of Richmond, Virginia. Valentine Richmond History Center

Gen Lee judging I prefer it still after — this is... during the War. It was made for me. I sent it... 1864 ... E.V. Vallentine

Edward V. Valentine's personal gelatin silver copy print of one of Julian Vannerson's "blockade" photographs of General Lee; copy made by George Cook of Richmond, Virginia, circa 1880. Donald A. Hopkins

federacy. The statuette was sold & found its way somewhere in Scotland. Edward V. Valentine.[17] (Appendix C)

Another of Valentine's personal copies of a Vannerson photograph was printed by the silver gelatin technique, which was not developed until the late 1870s. This copy is whole-plate size, printed on photographic paper which is blind-stamped on the lower border "COOK." Valentine scrawled across the tiny bottom margin:

General Lee sat for this picture during the War. It was made for me. I prefer it to all other photographs of mine. Edward V. Valentine.[18]

Period salt print copies of Vannerson photographs are uncommon. They are usu-

were all from the Blockade Images sitting and were copies made after Lee's death, bearing smudges and even gridlines indicating that they had been used to model some of the sculptor's later work. Each was slightly larger than whole-plate size, and one carried a notation on the back:

This photo is a copy from an original made during the War Between the States for me of Genl Robert E. Lee who sat for same. The original photo was made by Vannerson, Richmond, Va. & sent to me through the blockade to Berlin. I modeled from this a statuette of Genl Lee which was sent to the Liverpool Bazaar for the benefit of the Con-

An example of a small salt-print copy, unmarked, based on a photograph of General Lee made by Julian Vannerson in early 1864 in Richmond, Virginia. Howard McManus

ally very small and mounted on unmarked card mounts. However, Vannerson made a few larger (5¼ inches by 7¼ inches) salt print copies of at least one pose from this sitting.

These 1864 photographs of General Lee remained very popular for many years after the war. Many of these Vannerson photographs were copied for sale in the North and have United States revenue stamps on their verso.

Revenue Stamps and Photographs

For two years, from August 1, 1864, until August 1, 1866, the United States government imposed a taxation system to help pay for the war. Photographs, ambrotypes, daguerreotypes, or any "sun" pictures[19] were required to have a tax stamp affixed to the back of the image; exempted were photographs too small for the stamp to be affixed, in which case the purchaser paid five percent tax to the seller. The act required that the seller of the photograph cancel the stamp by initialing or marking

An example of a carte de visite copy of a Vannerson photograph produced by C. D. Fredricks of New York with a United States revenue stamp on the verso. Donald A. Hopkins

the stamp and dating it. The government did not produce revenue stamps specifically for photographs, so vendors used general proprietary revenue stamps. The amount of the tax (from one to more than five cents) depended on the price of the photograph.[20] As cartes de visite were often bought by the dozen for friends or family members, enough stamps were required to cover the cost of the group, and therefore all twelve photographs might not have a stamp affixed.

Cost

REQUIRED STAMP
LESS THAN 25 CENTS
2-CENT (BLUE/ORANGE)
25 TO 50 CENTS
3-CENT (GREEN)
50 CENTS TO $1
5-CENT (RED)
MORE THAN $1
5-CENT FOR EACH ADDITIONAL DOLLAR OR FRACTION THEREOF

Obviously, images made in the Confederate States during the war would not have such Federal stamps affixed to them. Any Lee image bearing its original revenue stamp certainly was not sold within the Confederacy; it was sold in the North between August 1864 and August 1866, or possibly in one of the Southern states between the war's end (spring 1865) and August 1866.

Another example of Vannerson's left profile image of Lee was pasted on a larger, relatively thin white card stock mount measuring 4¼ inches by 6½ inches. The publisher is unknown.

Photograph Card Mounts

During the Civil War, the most common size card for supporting the thin albumen

An example of a larger card mount, called a cabinet card, bearing an enhanced and vignetted copy of a photograph of General Lee, the original having been made by Julian Vannerson of Richmond, Virginia, in 1864. Donald A. Hopkins

paper prints of photographic images was the small carte de visite card measuring about 2⅜ inches by 4¼ inches. The larger, so-called "cabinet card," which measured 4¼ inches by 6½ inches, was not used in America until after 1866, but by 1885 had taken over most of the carte de visite's market. The cabinet card was basically a larger version of the carte de visite, retaining the photographer's imprint and exhibiting similar styles of decorative artwork on the card face or back. Like its predecessor, it consisted of a paper photographic print mounted on commercially produced card stock of standard size. The cabinet format was used for landscape views before it was adopted for portraiture. The majority of cabinet cards were albumen prints, but toward the end of the nineteenth century other types of photographic paper began to replace albumen paper. Gelatin papers were introduced in the 1870s and gained in popularity over the next 20 years. Cabinet cards were produced as late as 1924.

In addition to cabinet cards, post-Civil War photographs may be found mounted on one of several larger sized cards.

Larger Sized Photograph Card Mounts

Cabinet card (Imperial carte de visite)
    4¼" x 6½"
Victoria card
    3¼" x 5"
Promenade card
    4" x 7"
Boudoir card
    5" x 8½"
Imperial card
    12¾" x 17⅜"

Any Robert E. Lee photograph mounted on one of these larger cards was fabricated after the war.

Dating Larger Card Photographs

Several features can help determine when a larger card-mounted photograph was produced; however, these guidelines are not hard-and-fast rules, as there are many exceptions.

Sitter Pose
1866 – 1870:
The sitter is either seated or standing, but is shown full length (unless it is a copy of an earlier portrait photograph)
1870 – 1880:
The sitter is usually depicted closer up, not necessarily full length

Card Colors
1866 – 1880:
Lightweight, white card stock
1880 – 1890:
Different colors for face and back of cards
1882 – 1888:
Face of buff, matte-finished, with a back of creamy yellow, often glossy

Borders
1866 – 1880:
Red or gold rules, single and double lines
1884 – 1885:
Wide gold borders, more elaborate
1885 – 1892:
Gold-beveled edges
1889 – 1896:
Rounded corner rule of single line
1890 – 1892:
Metallic green- or gold-impressed border
1896:
Impressed outer border, without color

Corners
1866 – 1880:
Square, lightweight mounts
1880 – 1890:
Square, heavy board, often with scalloped sides

Photographer Imprint/Advertising
1866 – 1870:
Simple one or two lines, or none at all
1870 – 1900:
Gradually more elaborate, with artwork

Backdrop
1866 – 1868:
Relatively plain backdrop
1868 – 1900:
Increasingly fancy, painted and decorated backdrops

The "Floppy Tie" Images

Robert E. Lee had another photographic session, likely in Richmond, circa 1864. This resulted in the so-called "Floppy Tie" image because the image most frequently seen from this series shows Lee's bow tie to

One of three photographs made circa 1864 erro-neously attributed to John W. Davies of Rich-mond, Virginia, which shows General Lee's bow tie before the right side begins to droop downward. Valentine Richmond History Center

lating to these photographs, supposedly taken by Davies.

John W. Davies of Richmond was a stonemason who became a sheet music publisher and dealer during the war.[21] Collectors of Confederate imprints are familiar

One of three photographs made circa 1864 erroneously attributed to John W. Davies of Richmond, Virginia, which shows General Lee's bow tie just as its right side begins to droop downward. Valentine Richmond History Center

be dangling on its right side. Most author-ities and collectors, from the time of Roy Meredith's study until now, have firmly at-tributed these photographs to John W. Davies; but the basis for such attribution is elusive, at best.

These images appear very similar to one of the earlier Van-nerson images, dif-fering in that Lee is not wearing a vest (waistcoat) under his military jacket as he was in the earlier pho-tographs, and his beard is cropped a little more closely. He seems to be wearing the same jacket as in the Vannerson pho-tographs, but with a nar-rower bow tie. There are several puzzling aspects re-

with his sheet music, which carries his Richmond imprint, but a dili-gent search through hundreds of wartime photographs made in Richmond during the Civil War

One of three photographs made circa 1864 erroneously attributed to John W. Davies of Richmond, Vir-ginia, which shows General Lee's bow tie with the right side fully drooped downward. Stratford Hall has failed to turn up a single one with an imprint of Davies. In fact, no backmark known to have been in use by any Richmond photographer during the war has been found on any of these three views from this "Floppy Tie" photographic session. Many, if not most, are seen with no imprint at all. However, Davies' later postwar imprint, in use after he opened the "Lee Gallery" with his son William, is quite common and is often found on copies of these "Floppy Tie" photographs. Since this is certainly a wartime photograph of the General in his Confederate uniform, one must ask, who was the original photographer?

Vannerson was one of Richmond's most active photographers during the war, according to sales tax and license information. In fact, Vannerson may have been the only photographic artist operating in Richmond for most of 1864. All the while, Davies is not mentioned at all as a photographer in such records. Certainly, Davies and Vannerson developed a close business relationship shortly after the war ended, with the Vannerson studio being located upstairs above Davies' Music Exchange. Perhaps Vannerson made the original photographs during the war and, for whatever reason, did not put his imprint on them. This theory is not entirely unlikely. In postwar correspondence of 1867, Lee wrote that a carte de visite version of the "Floppy Tie" photograph which he was sending to an admirer had been made "during the war by Vannerson's Co., Richmond, Virginia."[22] Roy Meredith evidently was not cognizant that the Davieses, father and son, first opened the Lee Gallery in the postwar period rather than during the war. Their new studio was upstairs over their music store, the site recently vacated by Vannerson. Vannerson's location would certainly have made it convenient for John Davies and his son William to learn the craft of photography from the experienced artist.

Most examples of the three photographs from this session which have been found with any backmark at all have the postwar imprints of Vannerson and Jones, Vannerson and Levy, or the Davies' Lee Gallery, which later owned the Vannerson negatives. The Virginia Historical Society has a carte de visite of the "Floppy Tie" portrait with an old printed label on the verso reading: "Gen. R. E. Lee, from original negative in possession of Lee Gallery, Richmond, Virginia." This could lead anyone, including Roy Meredith, to conclude that J. W. Davies actually made the photograph; but in reality, Davies' collection of negatives at the Lee Gallery included Vannerson's wartime work, which likely included these three negatives. Wartime carte de visite copies of the original photograph have no imprint at all. The most logical conclusion is that the "Floppy Tie" photograph may well have been made by Vannerson, but definitely not by John W. Davies. Why Vannerson, if he indeed made these photographs, did not place his imprint on them during the war remains a mystery.

Meredith speculated that, because the most well-known view from this series of photographs shows the right tip of the General's bow tie drooping downward, whereas another version showed it less droopy, Mrs. Lee arranged for alteration of the original negative to a more pleasing image.[23] This is an interesting but doubtful possibility. Among other reasons, Mrs. Lee did not seem to have a particular aversion to the floppy tie, as she signed several presentation copies of this photograph after the war. Incidentally, she also noted in some of her ink presentations inscribed on the backs of these cartes de visite that "this photograph was made in the 3rd year of the War," which helps firm up the conclusion that it was taken in 1864, well before the Davies family opened their gallery.

The first view seems to have been made with the camera lens a little closer to Lee, since less of his torso and right arm are visible than in the next two exposures. Closer examination reveals other slight differences between the three images, besides the progressive drooping of the tie. Note the relative positions of the lower buttonholes on the lapel and the various creases in Lee's coat. For instance, the buttonholes on the left lapel shift slightly upward in the second and third images compared with the first, and there are differences in the wrinkles and creases in the right arm of Lee's jacket as well as very slight changes in the tilt of his head.

It is also clear from close examination of only the head and neck portions of these pictures that the three poses vary slightly from one another. Many students of Lee images seem not to have considered the first image—in which the ends of the tie are rigidly straight, actually pointing a little upward—as part of this sitting. However, even a casual examination shows the exact same uniform and hair and beard configuration in each. The slightly baggy eyes are also consistent. Slight variation in the tilt of Lee's head causes minute differences in the location of light reflected from his eyes. It is quite easy to see a minuscule but definite difference in the three poses between the relationship of the tip of

Cropped views of the three poses of the "Floppy Tie" series of photographs are presented to illustrate the differences in the relationship of the left end of General Lee's bow tie and the left lapel of his coat. Valentine Richmond History Center

the left side of the tie to the left lapel border. These photographs clearly represent three separate views taken at the same sitting.

The wet collodion process used to produce the glass negatives for these images required that the collodion remain wet throughout the entire process, which usually lasted no more than ten minutes. It appears that the photographer, following the customary procedures of the day, first set up his camera in position to take advantage of the natural light flooding the studio through windows or skylights, utilizing appropriate reflectors as needed. He then composed the image by positioning Lee exactly as he wanted. He made adjustments to the pose after peering—

through a removable focusing glass made of ground glass in the rear of his camera, on through the camera lens while he focused it—at a nearly motionless Lee. Meanwhile, in the darkroom, an assistant coated one side of the glass plate with collodion which had been made light-sensitive, then loaded it into a plate holder before passing it to the photographer. The photographer quickly replaced the focusing glass at the back of the camera with the sensitized negative plate and exposed the plate before the collodion could dry.

Ordinarily, a mid-nineteenth century photographer would develop an image, inspect the results, and, if not satisfied, adjust as necessary the lens position and focus, lighting, and exposure time. It seems that in this case the artist made three separate exposures over an undetermined period, perhaps quickly moving his lens a little further from Lee after the first exposure. The closer the subject was to the camera, the less exposure time was required.[24] If a single plate was used to capture three separate images, all in the brief time span before the plate became dry, there was little time to rearrange the General's pose between exposures. The progressive drooping of the tie seems to have been of little consequence to the photographer. Perhaps all other elements of the third exposure were so pleasing that he determined that this exposure would be "showcased" as the main product of this sitting, despite the drooping tie. It is the most common view encountered from this session.

It seems likely that these images were made using a "multiplying" camera that allowed the photographer to successively expose different parts of the same sensitized glass plate in order to make three different negatives. This could have been done either by rotating a lens in front of the plate for each exposure; or removing the caps from multiple lenses one after another in sequence; or by sliding the wet glass plate in its plate holder across the back of the camera behind a single lens in increments, so as to expose only part of the plate at a time.

It is not unreasonable to think that the General, impatient with the whole process, might have taken a deep breath or two or otherwise subtly shifted his position a tiny bit between the last two exposures. Interestingly, the Valentine Richmond History Center, which houses most of the Cook (Vannerson) negatives, carries notations on a print of the "Floppy Tie" photograph that one of the glass-plate negatives (not available for examination) "shows three separate views." This would indeed suggest the use of a multiplying camera. Knowledge of the size of the original negatives would help answer some of these questions. At any rate, this photographic sitting produced three separate negatives, either on one plate or three separate plates.

An advertisement in carte de visite format from the Lee Photographic Gallery in Richmond, Virginia, which used as a central medallion a well-known Vannerson portrait of General Lee.
Valentine Richmond History Center

John Woodburn Davies

John Woodburn Davies (1818-1883) was born in Liverpool, England. Though trained as a stonemason, he studied civil engineering. In 1848, he settled in Richmond, Virginia. Listed under "Stone and Marble works" in the 1860 Richmond Business Di-

rectory, he frequently placed advertisements in the Richmond newspapers. His business was located on 9th Street between Main and Franklin.[25] By 1861, he was exhibiting statuary and paintings in his gallery in Mechanic's Hall. Davies made many of the monuments found today in Hollywood Cemetery and in the Hebrew Cemetery in Richmond.[26] In March 1864, his warehouse/storehouse, along with his inventory of statuary and tools, were destroyed by fire, after which time he opened a "book and fancy store" adjacent to his storehouse.[27] By September 1864, he and his sons, William W. and George L. Davies, had opened the Richmond Music Exchange at the same location. His advertisements in wartime newspapers locate it at "188 Main Street, at P. H. Taylor's old stand."[28] Some of the Davies' advertisements listed their business as that of "lithographers and music publishers" or as a "book and music store"—but none as a photographer.[29] The imprint "J. W. Davies & Son" can be found on several pieces of Confederate sheet music.

The building which housed the Davies' business was destroyed or badly damaged in the Richmond fires of April 2-3, 1865. Their "elegant music establishment" reopened for business in November of that year with Vannerson and Jones, photographers, moving into a new studio above the Music Exchange.[30] As late as 1866, Richmond business directories listed Davies as a dealer in music, not as a photographer.[31]

Before April 1869, Vannerson sold his business, including his extensive archive of negatives, to the Davies family. The Davieses advertised on their cartes de visite "Lee Photographic Gallery – successor to Vannerson & Jones." John Davies' son, William W. Davies, worked with and later succeeded his father as proprietor.[32] In 1870, the business was firmly established as the Lee Photographic Gallery, described as "over the Richmond Music Exchange." One variety of their backmarks notes John W. Davies as "Superintendent" and another listed William D. Cooke in that position.

The Lee Gallery distributed an advertising carte de visite that had an oval portrait of the General in the center. This photograph was not the "Floppy Tie" image which has been erroneously attributed to John Davies, but a copy of a Vannerson portrait. The gallery operated until about 1891, when it was sold to George Cook, whose studio was located across the street at 913 East Main Street at the location previously occupied by David H. Anderson, and before that by Charles Rees.

The General's Last Wartime Photograph

The final wartime photograph of Robert E. Lee is the only one made during the war of the General on his horse Traveller.[33] It was probably taken on a street in Petersburg during the final days of the bloody conflict. Lee interrupted his duties long enough to briefly pose astride his horse, for some photographer unknown to us but probably known to Lee.

This photograph definitely appears to have been posed, and it seems unlikely that Lee would have taken time to pose for a pho-

tograph at this critical point in the war unless he was implored to do so by either his staff or an artist personally known to him. Daniel T. Cowell, who made the "In the Field" photographs of Lee, had left George Minnis in Richmond in the spring of 1864, evidently for Petersburg. Immediately after the war, he was working there with J. R. Rockwell. He was certainly already acquainted with Lee.

The glass-plate negative for this photograph is now owned by the Dementi Studio of Richmond, Virginia, which obtained it from the noted historian and Lee biographer Douglas Southall Freeman. A signed copy of this photograph was passed down through the Lee family and now belongs to the National Park Service.

While at Petersburg, General Lee on at least one occasion sent a female admirer a photograph, a practice he continued after the war on a much more frequent basis.[34]

Wartime Photographers of Petersburg, Virginia

Although the actual photographer of Lee and his horse is unknown, there were very few photographers operating in Petersburg as the war drew to a close, most having left before or during the protracted siege of the city. One who maintained his prewar address was James R. Rockwell of Rockwell's gallery. He was listed in the 1860 Petersburg census as a 22-year-old "artist" born in Virginia. His imprint is found on wartime images, recording his studio location at 13.5 Sycamore Street, Petersburg.[35] A well-known composite image of Lee and his staff published in 1866, the so-called "Military Medallion," bears the imprint of "Rockwell and Cowell, Petersburg." Rockwell had begun work on the composite of photographs which comprised the medallion as early as April 1865, immediately after the end of the war, confirming that he was still in business in Petersburg.[36] According to the 1866 Petersburg

An example of an uncommon photograph of General Lee mounted on Traveller that was made in Petersburg in the fall of 1864 by an unknown photographer, possibly J. R. Rockwell or Daniel Cowell.
Dementi Studio

City Directory, Daniel Cowell was sharing this same Sycamore Street address with Rockwell. This firm also sold a carte de visite copy of the Minnis and Cowell 1863 "In the Field" image of Lee that appeared as the centerpiece of the medallion. An example of this carte de visite bearing a revenue stamp and dated April 1866 confirms that Cowell and Rockwell were working together in Petersburg at that time.

Sycamore Street in Petersburg had become the hub of photographic activity in the city even before the war. Many of the photographers at one time or another worked out of studios at 13 Sycamore Street. During the month of November 1864, General Lee's headquarters was located at the Beasley House on High Street, a short ride of less than a mile from 13 Sycamore Street. He likely rode by the pho-

tographer's studio on his frequent visits into the city or en route to the siege lines.

As perhaps the sole active Southern photographer in Petersburg during late 1864, circumstances suggest quite strongly that James Rockwell, perhaps in conjunction with Daniel Cowell, made this photograph of Lee mounted on Traveller.

Notes
Chapter 6: In All His Martial Splendor

[1] British Colonel Arthur Fremantle describes Robert E. Lee in June 1863. – Ralston B. Lattimore, ed., *The Story of Robert E. Lee as Told in his own Words and those of his Contemporaries* (Washington, D.C., 1964), 54.

[2] Meredith, *The Face of Robert E. Lee*, 44.

[3] Elizabeth Gray Valentine, *Dawn to Twilight: Work of Edward V. Valentine* (Richmond, VA, 1929), 131.

[4] Mark D. Katz, "New Faces of Robert E. Lee," *Civil War Times Illustrated*, April 1983, 42-45.

[5] Meredith's book is copyrighted, as is his compilation of photographs, but he does not have copyright protection for the individual photographs he used, which were in the public domain when he produced his work.

[6] "It-Kha-Ka-Hang-Zhe, Standing Elk, Warrior, Yankton Sioux," in Chrysler Museum Collection, Object No. 9235. Norfolk, VA. http://collectiononline.chrysler.org/emuseum/view/objects/asitem/People

[7] Gorman, "Civil War Richmond" (Richmond, VA, 2008). http://www.mdgorman.com/Written_Accounts/newspaper

[8] Ruggles, *Photography in Virginia*, 50.

[9] Craig, "Julian Vannerson," in *Craig's Daguerreian Registry*. Ruggles, *Photography in Virginia*, 29.

[10] The "burnt district," so-called by contemporary newspapers, consisted of 80% of the business and industrial district of Richmond which was destroyed by the evacuation fires of April 1865.

[11] "Building in the Burnt District of Richmond," *The Norfolk Post*, July 13, 1865. http://chroniclingamerica.com/

[12] C. B. Richardson to Robert E. Lee, March 12, 1866, Leyburn Library, Washington and Lee University.

[13] James K. Caskie to Robert E. Lee, April 13, 1866, Leyburn Library, Washington and Lee University.

[14] Photographers Levy and Cohen of Philadelphia were in Richmond soon after its occupation photographing the "burnt district." They did not return to Philadelphia until September 1865. It is quite possible that Levy worked briefly with Vannerson. Gorman, "Civil War Richmond." Richmond, VA: Civil War Richmond, Inc., 2008. http://www.mdgorman.com/Photographs/levy&.htm

[15] Cowan's Auctions, "Libby Prison Presentation Photograph from a New Jersey Officer," catalog entry in *Western and Historical Americana* (Cincinnati, OH, June 24, 2009), Lot 188.

[16] Ruggles, *Photography in Virginia*, 84.

[17] Heritage Collectibles Auctions, "Sculptor Edward Valentine's Personal Vannerson Photographs of Robert E. Lee Used in Modeling his Famous Statue," catalog entry in *June 2007 Grand Format Civil War Auction* (Dallas, TX, June 25, 2007), Lot 74115.

[18] Author's collection.

[19] The quaint term "sun" pictures as used in the regulation implied all photographic techniques which required that the image be taken in the sunlight, either outdoors or through windows or skylights of a gallery.

[20] Darrah, *Cartes De Visite*, 87.

[21] Gorman, "Civil War Richmond" (Richmond, VA, 2008). http://www.mdgorman.com/Written_Accounts/newspaper

[22] Heritage Collectibles Auctions, "Autograph Letter Signed by Robert E. Lee accompanied by a Signed Carte De Visite of the General in a Confederate Uniform," catalog entry in *June 2007 Grand Format Civil War Auction* (Gettysburg, PA, June 24, 2007), Lot 72023.

[23] Meredith, *The Face of Robert E. Lee*, 52.

[24] D. van Monckhoven, *A Popular Treatise on Photography also a Description of, and Remarks on, the Stereoscope and Photographic Optics, Etc. Etc.*, trans. W. H. Thorntwaite (London, 1863), 48-55.

[25] Gorman, "Civil War Richmond" (Richmond, VA, 2008). http://www.mdgorman.com/Written_Accounts/newspaper

[26] Ibid.

[27] Ibid.

[28] Ibid.

[29] Ibid.

[30] Ibid.

[31] William J. Devine & Co., comp., *Richmond City Directory, 1866: Containing a business directory of all the persons engaged in business, classified according to the business: and a city register containing much useful information* (Richmond, VA, 1866), n.p.

[32] "Father, Daughter Dead," *Times Dispatch* [Richmond, VA], December 8, 1903, 2. http://chroniclingamerica.loc.gov/lccn/sn85038615/1903-12-08/ed-1/seq-2/

[33] Robert M. Pendleton, Traveller: *General Robert E. Lee's Favorite Greenbrier War Horse* (Victoria, British Columbia, Canada, 2005), front matter.

[34] Robert E. Lee to Miss Mary C. Jerdone, January 8, 1865, Leyburn Library, Washington and Lee University.

[35] The ".5" indicated that Rockwell's studio was on the second floor. This upstairs location was common for photographers, as they needed the extra illumination provided by skylights, with a northern exposure if possible.

[36] Trent, "Robert E. Lee," vol. 10, 61.

CHAPTER 7

WARTIME ORIGINAL "FROM LIFE" IMAGES OF R. E. LEE

"It is a good face: it is the face of a noble, noble, brave man."[1]

The most valuable Robert E. Lee photographs are prints made from unaltered, original, "from life" negatives produced as Lee sat for the photographic artist. This would be the "first generation" of the photograph. Only one such negative ever existed for each first-generation pose. Such a photographic print would have been the exact same size as the glass-plate negative exposed while the General sat motionless in front of the camera, perhaps reduced by a small amount trimmed from around the irregularly exposed edges of the developed photograph.

Certainly, a "from life" photographic print could be cropped to show only the head or torso of the General and still be considered as produced from the original negative. In such cases the representation of the subject's head or torso should be the exact same size as in the untrimmed "from life" negative. This type of severe cropping was occasionally done to separate the head and upper torso portions from the remainder of a larger picture in order for the portrait to fit the dimensions of a cabinet card.

Apparently, all of Lee's wartime portraits were originally made in sizes larger than carte de visite size. A wartime carte de visite of Lee, even if imprinted by one of his known "from life" photographers, is simply a copy made in small size for the mass market, not a "from life" image.[2] Furthermore, any photograph of Robert E. Lee wearing a uniform, complete with Confederate insignia, of a size greater than whole-plate size should not be considered a "from life" wartime image. It was possible, but very unlikely, that a solar enlargement[3] was made from an original negative of Robert E. Lee during the war. Wartime "from life" photographs of General Lee most likely were larger than a carte de visite, but no larger than whole-plate size.

When working in a studio, the photographer usually had at hand a large camera capable of exposing the relatively heavy whole-plate negatives. These were large enough to allow for artistic alterations or enhancements in the negative itself, or more commonly the first-generation print. Artistic embellishments of hair, beard, facial features, or clothing was very common in the nineteenth century, causing many later-generation images to look more like engravings than photographs—as well as to lose their "from life" status. In many cases, even the backdrop behind the subject was embellished to make it appear more elaborate.

If the photographic artist chose to work on his original, fragile, glass-plate negative to improve, enhance, or in any way modify it, he would risk irretrievably spoiling or breaking it. Therefore, in actual practice a print, or perhaps a few prints, were made from this original negative before any alterations were attempted, either in the negative or in the corresponding printed-out photograph. These photographs of Robert E. Lee would represent the only true "from life" examples of a particular pose and are exceedingly rare, in some cases now nonexistent.

Once the photographer had enhanced, "cleaned up," or otherwise altered his original negative or print to his satisfaction, he would photographically produce second-generation prints (if working from an altered negative) or a second-generation negative (if working from an altered print). Satisfactory prints to serve as specimens of his work in his gallery and for the marketplace could then be produced in large quantities. With the enhanced or "improved" second-generation negative at hand, the original negative produced while General Lee sat for the photograph was often set aside and forgotten, as the photographer had little reason to make additional prints from it.

Many of these later-generation prints are today erroneously called "from life" photographs. But unless a photograph of Robert E. Lee has the identifying imprint of the original photographer or that of one of the

original artist's successors in business who is known to have acquired the original negatives, that photograph cannot with certainty be considered a "from life" image. Richmond, Virginia, photographers made (with one possible exception) all known wartime "from life" images of Lee. As discussed in the previous chapter, the possible exception is the image of Lee on his horse Traveller, taken by an unknown photographer in Petersburg near the end of the war.[4] The three artists who are known to have made wartime photographs of Lee "from life" are George Minnis and Daniel T. Cowell working together, and Julian Vannerson. Not surprisingly, all photographs of Lee known to have been made during the war portray the General in uniform.

To reiterate a previous point, a vignetted photograph cannot be considered a "from life" image because by definition vignetting caused the subject to merge into the background, a procedure usually accomplished by masking a negative. Though possible, during this period in the Confederacy an original "from life" negative was rarely produced as a vignetted image by a modified camera lens while the subject sat for the photograph. None of the negatives of the known "from life" wartime photographs of Robert E. Lee were originally made as vignetted photographs. This is easily confirmed by the fact that all known wartime photographic poses of him exist in non-vignetted format; one cannot "un-vignette" a photograph. All vignetted images of Lee are later-generation modified copies.

Wartime glass-plate negatives of Lee made "from life" were most likely originally printed out by the albumen silver paper print technique. It is possible that Minnis or Vannerson used his original negatives to print out an occasional salt print, but for it to be considered original and "from life" it would have to bear the photographer's imprint and be the same size as the original negative. Most Confederate salt prints do not have a photographer's imprint and many are quite small, even gem-size.[5]

A complete collection of these truly original photographs of Lee made through the spring of 1865 would include an example from each of the eleven poses from his five known wartime photographic sessions. These eleven "from life" images are treasures eagerly sought by museums and collectors. Unfortunately, most of the photographs of Robert E. Lee currently marketed at high prices as "from life" are no such thing. They are not the proper size, or they have been altered by vignetting or

other enhancement, or do not bear the imprint of the original artist or his successor in business.

It is fitting to close these chapters on Robert E. Lee's wartime photographs with a little-known sidelight of history.

"On the last day of his life, at family breakfast at the White House on April 14, 1865, Mrs. Lincoln's seamstress recalled that Captain Robert Lincoln, just returned from the front bursting with news of the Appomattox surrender ceremony, showed his father a photograph of Lee. Studying it, the President is said to have remarked, "It is a good face: it is the face of a noble, noble, brave man."[6]

Notes

Chapter 7: Wartime Original "From Life" Images of R. E. Lee

[1] Abraham Lincoln, upon seeing a picture of Robert E. Lee. – Mark E. Neely, Jr., and Harold Holzer, *The Lincoln Family Album: Photographs from the Personal Collection of a Historic American Family* (New York, NY, 1990), 92-93.

[2] A photograph of a different size than the original negative plate cannot be a "from life" photograph.

[3] A solar enlargement resulted from sunlight being directed through a lens which condensed the light. The light was then projected through a photographic negative onto a piece of sensitized paper larger than the negative itself.

[4] Most likely James R. Rockwell and Daniel Cowell of Rockwell Gallery, Petersburg, VA.

[5] In many cases in the Confederacy salt prints were produced simply to conserve chemicals and paper.

[6] Neely and Holzer, *Lincoln Family Album*, 92-93. Marshall Fishwick states that Lincoln said "It is a good face. I am glad the war is over," in *Lee After the War* (New York, NY, 1963), 33.

ROBERT E. LEE'S POSTWAR PHOTOGRAPHERS

"I have seen many pictures of General Lee but never one that conveyed a correct impression of his appearance."[1]

During the years following the war, many photographers and publishers, especially throughout the South, continued to produce pictures of General Lee. Most of these pictures represented Lee during wartime. As time passed, a few photographers made new, original photographs of the graying veteran, usually in civilian attire, but sometimes in his old military jacket shorn of insignia. Lee sat for photographers, both North and South, quite frequently during the last four and a half years of his life.

Northern Postwar Photographers of Lee

At least three Northern photographers, and possibly four, photographed Lee after the war. The first was Mathew Brady of Washington, D.C.; the second was Alexander Gardner of Washington, D.C.; and the third was Henry Pollock of Baltimore. Palmer L. Perkins of Baltimore was possibly a fourth.

Southern Postwar Photographers of Lee

Southern photographers who made postwar images included Michael Miley of Lexington, Virginia; Adam H. Plecker, with his traveling gallery; Charles R. Rees of Richmond; David H. Anderson of Richmond and Norfolk, Virginia, and White Sulphur Springs, West Virginia; and David J. Ryan of Savannah, Georgia. Quite possibly N. S. Tanner and his associate James H. Van Ness of Lynchburg, Virginia, also photographed Lee. One enigmatic set of poses was possibly made in Norfolk, perhaps in the studio of D. H. Anderson in association with Julian Vannerson.

Reporting in October 1865 on the destruction caused by the evacuation fire in Richmond earlier that year, the *Philadelphia Photographer* noted that "it is a singular fact that with but one single exception, every photograph gallery in Richmond was destroyed. Every poor photographer forced to vacate and change his base."[2] Julian Vannerson was apparently the one Richmond photographer who was able to move back into his studio soon after the fire and not "change his base."

Several photographers relocated to Virginia after the war and either started out in business on their own or purchased a business, including negatives, from retiring or relocating photographers. Others simply relocated within the state of Virginia, often with new associates. In this manner some of the original "from life" negatives made of Lee during the war became the legitimate property of artists and publishers other than the original photographer. An imprint from any of their studios on a Robert E. Lee photograph, even one showing the General in uniform, indicates that the photograph was printed after the war.

Localities

The more familiar of these photographers or publishers who established businesses in **Richmond and its environs** and copied existing images of Lee or produced new photographs of Lee include:

• **David H. Anderson:** Originally of New York, Anderson traveled in the South and West until he settled in Richmond, Virginia, from 1866 until 1880. His studio was located at 121 Main Street, but in late 1866 the street numbering system was revamped, changing his address to 1311 Main Street. He marked some of his cartes de visite "Anderson and Co. Photographic Art Palace, old no. 121, new no. 1311, opposite Mitchell and Tyler's." Later his advertisements mentioned only the 1311 Main Street address.[3] At some point, he operated a studio at 913 Main Street, Richmond. He also worked out of studios in Norfolk, Virginia, and White Sulphur Springs, West Virginia.[4]

• **George S. Cook:** Relocating from Charleston, South Carolina, in 1880, Cook bought out D. H. Anderson (for $3,000) and imprinted some of his early work "George S. Cook, successor to D. H. Anderson, Richmond, Virginia." Cook acquired over 20,000 glass-plate negatives that Anderson had produced from his studios in Richmond and the Tidewater region of Virginia.[5] Cook apparently never made a "from life" photograph of Lee.

• **"Lee Photographic Gallery:"** In about 1870, John W. Davies and his son, photographers and sheet music dealers of Richmond, named their new studio "The Lee Photographic Gallery." Contrary to previous accounts, John W. Davies probably never made a "from life" photograph of Lee.

In **Petersburg**, Virginia, several studios were reopened after the cessation of hostilities, and a few new artists moved into the city. Some photographers with established galleries in Richmond opened branch operations in "the Cockade City" (Petersburg).[6] Some of their names associated with copies of Robert E. Lee photographs include the following:

• **Walter G. R. Frayser:** Frayser had originally come to Petersburg in 1852. During the war and until about 1868, he was in Richmond working with C. R. Rees and E. J. Rees, after which he returned to Petersburg.

• **G. W. Minnis:** He originally came to Petersburg in 1857, working in various locations on Sycamore Street. He set up a studio in Richmond which operated during the war. By 1871, he was working in Petersburg in a gallery listed as "Rees and Minnis."

- **Edwin (Edward) J. Rees:** He was first noted in Petersburg on Sycamore Street in 1859, associated with J. W. Walden. He worked with C. R. Rees and W. G. R. Frayser in Richmond during the war and early postwar period. In 1878, he was working in Petersburg.

- **Charles Richard Rees:** After working in Richmond during and immediately after the war, in 1871 he had a studio on Sycamore Street in Petersburg.

- **J. R. Rockwell** (perhaps the same as Joseph E.): He originally came to Petersburg in 1854 and maintained his studio location on Sycamore Street throughout the war. In September 1865, he advertised that he was now associated with D. T. Cowell.

Lexington, Virginia, home of the Robert E. Lee family, had only a small number of active photographers during the first few years after the war:

- **Joseph Kelly:** This artist was not well known as a photographer, but he did sell copies of at least one postwar photograph of Lee.[7]

- **James L. McCown:** An ex-Confederate who, in late 1866, worked for Michael Miley. McCown evidently later set up his own studio.

- **Michael Miley:** He is the best-known postwar photographer of Robert E. Lee. He began operation at the end of 1866 or early 1867 and took several "from life" photographs of the General, the only photographer with a studio in Lexington to do so. He also made copies of almost all known Lee photographs.

- **Adam Plecker:** He never set up a permanent studio in Lexington, but in the fall of 1866 he did take several well-known pictures of Lee and his family while his traveling gallery was at Lexington and Rockbridge Baths.

In **Lynchburg**, Virginia, perhaps the best-known studio was that of Tanner and Van Ness:

- **N. S. Tanner:** As early as 1856, he had an ambrotype gallery in Lynchburg, where he remained active for several years after the war.

- **James H. Van Ness:** This Confederate veteran joined Tanner shortly after the war. He later began to travel as an itinerate photographer.

Unattributed Photographs

For a few of Robert E. Lee's postwar photographs there is only tentative attribution to any particular artist, and in some cases not even that. In such cases no exact date is assigned to the resulting photographs, so they are simply sorted by commonality of wardrobe, studio props, and the physical appearance of Lee at the time.

This author has taken a fresh view of this small group of photographs and has developed some new perspectives by using information only recently available, including the study of details of photographs bought and sold at recent auctions. Correlating such information with Lee's travel itinerary was also helpful. In many cases, the opinions expressed in this volume about such images are at variance with conclusions of earlier students of Lee photographs.

Notes

Chapter 8: Robert E. Lee's Postwar Photographers

[1] John Sergeant Wise, *The End of an Era* (Boston & New York, 1899), 341-342.

[2] Edward L. Wilson, ed., "Our Picture," in *Philadelphia Photographer* (Philadelphia, PA, October 1865), 170.

[3] John M. Allan, ed., "D. H. Anderson," advertisement in *The Southern Planter and Farmer*, January 1870, 27.

[4] A photographer named Addison A. Knox had in his early years been "in the South working under D. H. Anderson at Richmond, Norfolk, and White Sulphur Springs." – T. Dixon Tennant, "Editor's Table," *Wilson's Photographic Magazine*, March 1909, 144.

[5] Kocher and Dearstyne, *Shadows*, 249. The Tidewater region of Virginia is watershed which drains through various rivers and streams into the Chesapeake Bay or the Atlantic Ocean. The area encompasses Norfolk, Richmond, and continues northward to the Arlington/Alexandria area.

[6] Since the War of 1812, Petersburg has sometimes been called the "Cockade City" because of cockades worn as part of the uniform of the Petersburg Volunteers.

[7] Barbara Crawford and Royster Lyle, Jr., *Rockbridge County Artists and Artisans* (Charlottesville, VA, 1995), 45-46.

CHAPTER 9

A WARRIOR TRANSFORMED

"As fine-looking a man as one would wish to see, of perfect figure and strikingly handsome."[1]

The renowned Mathew Brady of Washington, D.C., and New York made the earliest and perhaps the most well-known of the postwar photographic images of Robert E. Lee. He made these photographs in mid-April 1865, soon after the General returned to Richmond following his surrender of the Army of Northern Virginia at Appomattox Courthouse, Virginia. Brady used a door at the rear of Lee's rented house as a backdrop. General Lee posed somewhat reluctantly alongside his son G. W. Custis Lee and his longtime aide-de-camp Walter Taylor. Three of these now-classic photographs show the war-weary Lee standing and three are posed in sitting positions. These are the last photographs to show Lee in full military uniform, including the brass buttons with Confederate insignia. A Federal regulation soon made display of any Confederate symbols or insignia unlawful. General Lee appeared "Well proportioned, strong knit, erect, with beautifully proportioned features, small feet, and expressive hands. Just under six feet tall he weighed about one hundred and seventy pounds. His large head (in circumference twenty three and one half inches) was marked by brown eyes, prominent brows, and wide temples and sat on a strong neck. His narrow hips supported a massive torso so that he looked larger than he actually was. Agile and graceful, he was often likened to Apollo by those who saw him in action."[2]

A local newspaper described Brady's work: "General Lee and Staff – or rather those who accompanied him to Richmond – were yesterday photographed in a group by Mr. Brady, of New York. Six different sittings were then taken of General Lee, each in a different posture, and all were pronounced admirable pictures."[3]

A few days later, the same newspaper published another article about Mathew Brady's photographs. This report gave an extensive, detailed list of photographs and stereoscopic views taken by Brady during his recent trip to Virginia, but did not mention the Lee photographs. It also noted that all the photographs taken were whole-plate size.[4] Since all images listed in this newspaper article were either whole-plate size or stereoscopic views, one could infer that the original negative plate size for these Lee images was also whole-plate size or larger.

The original negative—of a pose of Lee standing with his right hand on a chair and hat in his left hand—was evidently lost or broken

Pose 1
One of six poses of General Lee taken by Mathew Brady of New York and Washington, D.C., in mid-April 1865 at Richmond, Virginia, which were originally made in a large format of about 9" x 11." Library of Congress

long ago. A faded copy of the original image occasionally surfaces, usually trimmed to an oval shape. The more common, though still scarce, version of this "lost negative" image has an entirely altered background. A large-format version, trimmed to an 8-inch by 6-inch oval and which bears Brady's imprint as well as a 5-cent revenue stamp, is considered a "from life"

Pose 2
One of six poses of General Lee taken by Mathew Brady of New York and Washington, D.C., in mid-April 1865 at Richmond, Virginia, which were originally made in a large format of about 9" x 11." Library of Congress

M. B. Brady & Co.   Entered according to Act of Congress by M. B. Brady & Co. in the year 1866, in the Clerk's Office of the District Court for the District of Columbia.

GEN'L ROBT. E. LEE AND STAFF.   Washington, D. C.

Pose 3
One of six poses of General Lee taken by Mathew Brady of New York and Washington, D.C., in mid-April 1865 at Richmond, Virginia, which were originally made in a large format of about 9" x 11." Library of Congress

photograph. The stamp indicates that this photograph was sold before August 31, 1866, for between 50 cents and one dollar.

An image of Lee standing alone in front of the door was so similar to another view that Brady took at this session that they were thought to be the same until 1983, when it was realized that Lee's position in relationship to the paneling on the door was different in the two images.

Pose 4

The rarest of six poses of General Lee taken by Mathew Brady of New York and Washington, D.C., in mid-April 1865 at Richmond, Virginia, is shown here as original and unaltered. Donald A. Hopkins

Pose 4, altered
The rarest of six poses of General Lee taken by Mathew Brady of New York and Washington, D.C., in mid-April 1865 at Richmond, Virginia, is shown here with totally altered background. Donald A. Hopkins

Pose 5
One of six poses of General Lee taken by Mathew Brady of New York and Washington, D.C., in mid-April 1865 at Richmond,
Virginia, which were originally made in a large format of about 9" x 11", often confused with "Pose 6," both of which show
Lee standing in slightly different positions in front of a paneled door. National Archives and Records Administration

Version one shows Lee centered directly in front of the cross-shaped panels of the door, while version two shows the cross panels in the door behind his right shoulder.[5] Even though the details of these two pictures are nearly identical, there are enough differences

Pose 6
One of six poses of General Lee taken by Mathew Brady of New York and Washington, D.C., in mid-April 1865 at Richmond, Virginia, which were originally made in a large format of about 9" x 11", often confused with "Pose 5," both of which show Lee standing in slightly different positions in front of a paneled door. Library of Congress

between them to rule out the possibility that they are photographs made simultaneously by a stereographic camera.

A very interesting recent discovery underscores the importance of examining old photographs from different perspectives. One never knows what might have previously gone unnoticed in spite of intense scrutiny by several generations of historians and collectors. At a seminar on Civil War photography in October 2005, during a reenactment of the taking of Brady's photographs, an examination of high-resolution enlargements of Brady's work revealed a startling surprise. A bit of unionist graffiti chalked upon a brick adjacent to the door spelled the word "Devil!" This offensive scrawl was removed at some point during the photographic session.[6] During the postwar period, Mathew Brady encountered an increasingly difficult financial situation. He tried to produce and market a series of lantern slides[7] entitled "War

Unionist graffiti spelling the word "devil" scrawled on the brick wall backdrop of the Brady photographs was discovered in 2005. Library of Congress

A rare lantern slide of "Pose 6" on a glass plate 4" x 3½" by Mathew Brady of New York and Washington, D.C. Donald A. Hopkins

for the Union," but they were not as successful as he might have wished. Only a few sets, each of which contained a copy of Brady's "Pose 6" of General Lee standing in front of the door, were produced. This particular image in its lantern-slide format, even though a copy image, is one of the rarest of all Robert E. Lee photographic presentations.

According to information from the Library of Congress in Washington, D.C., Brady entered his copyright registration for this group of photographs on April 13, 1865. Brady's images from this photographic session have been copied and recopied in all sizes and formats; they have been cropped, vignetted, and otherwise altered for years. The original, "from life" photographs were in a large format, larger than whole-plate size. All smaller sizes are simply later-generation copies.

The Brady Negatives

During the war, many of Mathew Brady's Civil War images were published by E. & H. T. Anthony, who came into possession of Brady negatives as compensation for photographic equipment and supplies. Brady later transferred several thousand additional original, glass-plate negatives and copy negatives to Anthony. In 1875, Brady auctioned some original negatives and copies of negatives that eventually became the property of the War Department. By the turn of the century, most of the Brady material that remained in the hands of Anthony and Company, including many of his wartime negatives, had been placed in storage. In 1902, Anthony's successor in business, Anthony and Scovill (later abbreviated to Ansco), sold about 18,000 of the Brady negatives, mostly portraits, originals and copies, to Frederick Hill Meserve.

Meserve spent the rest of his life working with the collection, printing at least 8,000 different images for a very limited number of copies of "Historic Portraits." In 1981, when Meserve's family finally put his collection up for sale, the National Portrait Gallery acquired more than 5,000 negatives for the Smithsonian Institution, nearly all of them studio portraits. The negatives from the Anthony Company's massive 1,100 stereoscopic view series which bore the same title as Brady's lantern slide set "War for the Union," was released in the spring of 1865. It included several hundred of Brady's most important documentaries of the battlefields. Negatives for this series became grouped with Alexander Gardner's negatives by the 1880s and went through several owners before being purchased by the Library of Congress in 1944. Yet others of Brady's negatives passed to his postwar assistant and nephew, Levin Handy, whose descendants later sold them to the government.

One of the more unique and fanciful portraits of Robert E. Lee is a blending of photography and painting. It is derived from one of Brady's April 1865 images showing the General seated, holding his hat in his lap. This 11-inch by 15-inch colored pastel rendition was described at auction as a colored photograph of Robert E. Lee seated in the library at Appomattox Courthouse. It is signed "Bendann." However, contrary to the auction catalog description, the surrender formalities held at Appomattox took place in a private home, the McLean House. Lee likely never entered the courthouse, and if he did it is doubtful that it contained the extensive library pictured. As noted earlier, the Bendann brothers of Baltimore were well-known photographers who early in the war published the first of the "doctored" images showing Lee in the uniform of a Virginia colonel. David Bendann signed this picture. He may simply have painted over a Brady photograph and replaced the background to make General Lee appear to be seated in a library.

A unique pastel rendering derived from one of Brady's April 1865, photographs showing General Lee with a fanciful backdrop by artist and photographer David Bendann of New York and Baltimore circa 1870. Donald A. Hopkins

The Military Medallion

A short time after the surrender of Lee's Army of Northern Virginia, a composite image of Lee and 12 of his staff, using wartime images of each subject, was marketed as the "Military Medallion." Originally made in a very large format suitable for framing, it was re-photographed into carte de visite size and sold by the thousands. These were available as early as December 1865, judging by the cancellation dates on revenue stamps affixed to some, although photographers Rockwell and Cowell of Petersburg did not obtain the copyright until 1866. Lee's image in the center is a variant of the familiar Minnis and Cowell 1863 image which was probably made at Lee's headquarters near Fredericksburg.

According to Major Giles B. Cooke (Number 12 in the composite):

An example of the original large format, 12" x 14" oval, "Military Medallion" made by Rockwell and Cowell of Petersburg, Virginia, in 1865. Donald A. Hopkins

changed. This military medallion was devised by the photographer Rockwell during General Lee's stay at Richmond in April, 1865.[8]

James R. Rockwell

James R. Rockwell was in business in Petersburg before the Civil War and he continued operating the Rockwell gallery during and after the war. If a photographer from Petersburg made the photograph of General Lee mounted on Traveller during the final months of the war, the artist was quite likely James Rockwell or his assistant Daniel T. Cowell.

In 1865, Cowell, who had been George W. Minnis' chief operator in Richmond for eight years, joined Rockwell at his gallery in Petersburg. In 1867, Minnis also joined Rockwell as a photographer. In about 1880, Charles R. Rees was working as a photographer at the gallery, and by 1888 had taken over the business.

In addition to the Military Medallion, the gallery also sold carte de visite-size copies of Lee's wartime, "In the Field" photograph that was most likely made originally by Cowell.

These twelve members of General Robert E. Lee's staff surrendered with him at Appomattox Court House, and with him signed a parole drawn up by Grant, to the effect that they would not take up arms against the United States until or unless they were ex-

A carte de visite of a variation of a photograph made by Alexander Gardner of Washington, D.C., in February 1866 which is actually cropped from a full sitting pose which is labeled "Pose 1" for the purposes of this manuscript.
Donald A. Hopkins

For many years it was unclear just how many photographs Alexander Gardner made of Robert E. Lee in early 1866. According to a biographer of Gardner, he took at least four separate exposures. Gardner copyrighted his photographs of General Lee about three weeks after they were taken, on March 7, 1866.

GENERAL ROBERT E. LEE.
Entered according to act of Congress, in the year 1866, by A. Gardner, in the Clerk's Office of the District Court of the District of Columbia.

Alexander Gardner's Magnificent Photographs

During the early Reconstruction period, General Lee was subpoenaed to a United States Senate hearing to be held in February 1866 in Washington, D.C. While there from February 16-19, he visited the photographic gallery of Alexander Gardner. This well-known artist had earlier been an associate in Mathew Brady's studio. Gardner became interested in large-size photographs while working with Brady, and was famous for his outdoor views and stereo views taken during the war.

Full sitting pose photograph made originally by Alexander Gardner of Washington, D.C., in February 1866 as an imperial size photograph which for purposes of this manuscript is labeled "Pose 1."
Library of Congress

His copyright application titled his pictures of Lee as "R. E. Lee no. 1-4."[9] It has now been confirmed that at least four separate poses were indeed taken during this sitting.

One of the most commonly seen variations of these poses is a right oblique view of Lee's upper torso. Careful examination of this image alongside "Pose 1," showing Lee seated, reveals that this particular photograph is not a separate "from life" pose but simply a cropped and vignetted Pose 1. Among other details of similarity, Lee's

tie projects slightly across his right lapel in only these two of Gardner's views. Since it is not a separate pose, it probably was not one of the original poses 1-4 that Gardner copyrighted. This variation sometimes bears Gardner's copyright notation, but it is quite common to find it unmarked or only with Gardner's imprint on the verso. When his copyright is found on this picture, it likely applies to the cropped portion from the original photograph, not its presentation as a vignetted view.[10]

Another full sitting pose photograph made originally by Alexander Gardner of Washington, D.C., in February 1866 as an imperial size photograph which for purposes of this manuscript is labeled "Pose 2." Museum of the Confederacy

Another pose showing the General in a sitting position, here labeled "Pose 2," was also taken. The differences in the position of Lee's hands and legs in these two seated poses were pointed out in 1983 by author Mark Katz.[11]

The "Pose 3" was not correctly attributed until 1983, when a Gardner copyrighted carte de visite was properly identified, again by Mark Katz. It also is more often found with only Gardner's backmark or no imprint at all, but is occasionally found with his copyright notation.

During the past few years, a large, imperial-sized image, 16 inches by 18 inches, still in its original period oval frame, was placed on the market by a well-known museum consultant.[12] Significantly, this portrait bears an Alexander Gardner copyright notation, dated 1866, across the bottom of the image. Gardner fre-

An example of a right profile view of General Lee taken by Alexander Gardner of Washington, D.C., in February 1866, which bears a Gardner backmark, for the purpose of this manuscript labeled "Pose 3." Virginia Historical Society

rare photograph firmly establishes that Alexander Gardner did indeed make a fourth photograph as part of his 1866 session with Lee in Washington, D.C.

This most recently identified pose is an almost right profile, but with a slight turn to the right, enough to see the lateral edge of Lee's left eye socket. Thus, this particular pose is basically a right profile image of the General, but not as sharply profiled as "Pose 3." It is quite uncommon in any format. It is usually attributed to Michael Miley, as it is most often seen heavily enhanced and bearing Miley's imprint.

The image described and pictured in the museum consultant's catalog is no longer accessible. No high-resolution photograph of the original is available. It is shown here as it appeared in the catalog, still in its oval-shaped frame, alongside an exact copy of the same picture which was found at the United States Army Heritage and Educa-

quently placed copyright notations on his larger photographs, perhaps as a reaction to having so much of his earlier work for Mathew Brady credited to his employer. This

not mention any of the Alexander Gardner photographs! The impact of Roy Meredith's study on later historians and curators is illustrated by the fact that the Virginia Historical Society has a carte de visite copy of "Pose 3," signed by the General, with Gardner's imprint on the back, and yet

tion Center in Carlisle, Pennsylvania.

Speculation has surrounded Gardner's sharp right profile view, "Pose 3," since 1947, when Roy Meredith published his work on Lee photographs. Meredith opined that this view was the work of Miley of Lexington, Virginia. However, in a glaring, almost unbelievable, omission, Meredith's book did

the original photograph is still attributed to Miley! Meredith felt that both of these right profile photographs, "Pose 3" and "Pose 4," were made at the same time by the same artist who was, in his opinion, Michael Miley. They indeed were made by the same artist at the same session—but the original photographer was Alexander Gardner, not Miley.

Michael Miley seems to have copied any other photographers' pictures of Lee that he could obtain. Examples of poses from each of Lee's prewar as well as his wartime photographic sittings carry Miley's own imprint or backmark. He also copied poses from Brady's 1865 postwar sitting even though Brady had copyright protection. There is no reason to believe Miley would have had any scruples against copying Alexander Gardner's work.

Subtle differences between two versions of "Pose 3" have led some students of Lee photographs to conclude that these two photographs were made by different photographers. However, the difference is actually more apparent than real. Close examination shows that Gardner's backmarked "Pose 3"

was slightly altered by blurring the detail between the General's chin and the top of his left shoulder. Otherwise the photographs are identical, even down to the wrinkles in the right lapel of his coat.

Gardner's carte de visite prints of these images occasionally bear the notation, "Entered according to Act of Congress in the year 1866, by A. Gardner, in the Clerk's Of-

An oval shaped presentation of Alexander Gardner's 1866 photograph as enhanced by Michael Miley of Lexington, Virginia, in about 1870.
Virginia Historical Society

A vignetted carte de visite example of Alexander Gardner's original 1866 photograph which bears his imprint presented for comparison with Michael Miley's later enhanced version of the same photograph. Virginia Historical Society

An example of the backmark used by Alexander Gardner from 1864-66. Virginia Historical Society

fice of the District Court, of the District of Columbia." The presence of revenue stamps on the back of some of Gardner's photographs from this sitting prove that they were sold before August 1866, before Michael Miley even had a studio of his own. Gardner's backmark that he used in early 1866, at the time these portraits were made, even had an imprinted frame within which he could place a revenue stamp.

It seems clear that, although Michael Miley's later enhancements and altered pre-sentations of these Gardner photographs represent his work, the original "from life" photographs must be credited to Gardner.

Within about three weeks of arriving back at Lexington from Washington, Lee found himself signing large numbers of these new photographs for friends, family, and to be sold for charitable causes.[13] This made it necessary for him to order additional copies from Gardner.

On April 10, 1866, Gardner had written:

Your favor of the 6th inst to hand this morning. From its tenor I infer you have not received a package of fifty cards assorted sent by mail within ten days after I sent the Box. A portion of them were without the imprint. I shall have 100 made & mounted without any imprint presuming you will prefer them so. When you wish any more let me know without sending any money. . . .[14]

On April 25, 1866, Lee replied:

I recd some days since your letter of the 10th with the profile photographs I requested on the 6th Inst: Since then I have rec'd the package, which you mention having previously sent, for which I am very much obliged. Please also accept my thanks for your kind offer to have prepared & mounted without the imprint, 100 of the same for me. I would prefer them in that way. They are much liked, & I wish to send some to the South & West, to friends who desire. . . .[15]

A carte de visite example of the photograph of Mrs. Robert E. Lee (Mary Custis Lee) made by Adam Plecker in Lexington, Virginia, in late 1866. Washington and Lee University

What was in the "box" that Gardner sent to the General, separate from the cartes de visite? Perhaps the answer lies in a very interesting article published in 1922, written by the photographer Adam H. Plecker. He recalled that he had traveled to the Lee residence in Lexington in the early fall of 1866 to photograph the invalided Mrs. Lee. He wrote:

The first thing I noticed on entering Mrs. Lee's room was a life-sized photo of the General, twenty-two by twenty-four, used as a screen to hide the fireplace. I remarked "Why, Mrs. Lee, why do you use that nice photo of the General in that way?" She laughed very heartily and said "It is the best use I can make of it, and it fitted very snugly in that space." This picture was in profile, a very fine photograph made by a Washington City photographer and they are very rare, the negative having gotten broken before many prints were struck off.[16]

It is quite likely that the "box" Gardner sent to General Lee in April 1866, in addition to the packages of cartes de visite, contained the large-format profile view which became Mrs. Lee's fire screen. Plecker's statement that the "negative [of the profile photograph making up the fire screen] having gotten broken before many prints were struck off" may explain why Gardner's "4th pose" is so rarely seen in its original, unenhanced version.

Michael Miley likely assisted Plecker with making the photographs of Mrs. Lee in her home, as he was employed by Plecker at the time. If so, he would certainly have noticed the large Fire Screen portrait of the General. With his penchant for photographing all things related to the Lee family, why would he not copy this impressive portrait?

In his book *The Face of Robert E. Lee in Life and in Legend*, Roy Meredith interprets Adam Plecker's account differently. He states that the portrait described by Plecker as making up the fire screen was the image Mathew Brady made in April 1865, showing Lee in uniform seated on his back porch in Richmond which revealed the left profile of his face. This picture is by no means rare, and there is no suggestion that the original negative was broken; in fact, it still exists in the Library of Congress. As noted earlier, however, nowhere in his book does Meredith describe the Gardner photographs at all! By excluding the Gardner profile views, indeed the Brady image would be the only profile made by an artist from Washington up to that time, thus leading to Meredith's conclusion. However, Alexander Gardner was also from Washington, and is now known to have taken two different profile views of Lee. For the Fire Screen photograph to appear "life sized" to Plecker, measuring 22" x 24," it must have been a "mammoth" or imperial-size photograph. Gardner specialized in such photographs. It seems most likely that this was the upper torso view of General Lee as in Gardner's work, rather than a full-seated view as in Brady's work. (Appendix D)

On April 15, 1867, in a letter to Reverend William C. Greene, Lee expressed a very favorable view of Gardner's work: "I have the houner [sic] to state in reply to your note of the 11 ulto; that I know of no good full sized photograph of Mr. Davis & Genl Beauregard. The best large one I have seen of myself is by Gardner of Washington City; a profile likeness. I enclose a small one taken during the war by Vannerson & Co., Richmond, Vir."[17] As noted in this correspondence, the General was quite fond of one of these profile views.

Incidentally, enclosed in this letter to Reverend Greene was a signed copy of a vignetted wartime "Floppy Tie" image, until recently attributed to John W. Davies. This carte de visite had a Vannerson and Jones backmark and a revenue stamp dated June 1865, indicating that it was an early postwar copy of the wartime photograph originally produced, according to the General himself, by Vannerson and Co.—not Davies. The revenue stamp provides additional evidence that the "Floppy Tie" photographs were sold to General Lee by Vannerson, well before the Davies family operated a photographic gallery.[18]

Alexander Gardner

Alexander Gardner was born in 1821 in Scotland. As a teenager he worked as an apprentice jeweler in Glasgow, later becoming a newspaper reporter and editor.

Gardner became enamored with socialist ideas and began to work toward developing a commune-type community in the United States. In 1850, he traveled with a small group to New York, where he remained while his brother moved on to Iowa to establish a cooperative community. Alexander soon returned to Scotland to raise money and recruit additional members for the commune.

Gardner saw some of Mathew Brady's photographic work in London, and at some point became acquainted with the celebrated American photographer himself. Gardner, who had spent his spare time in Scotland studying science, quite naturally became interested in photography. In 1856, he immigrated with his family to New York. Losing interest in the Iowa commune, he became Brady's assistant for the next two years before becoming manager of Brady's Washington, D.C., gallery. In the 1850s, Brady's eyesight had begun to deteriorate, and he relied heavily on Gardner to run the business. Gardner worked in this capacity until 1861, quickly developing a reputation as an outstanding portrait photographer.

Gardner specialized in making what became known as imperial photographs. These large prints (17 by 20 inches) were very popular, and Brady was able to sell them for between $50 and $750, depending on the amount of retouching with India ink required.

After the outbreak of the war in 1861, Gardner continued working for Brady's studio for a short period and is thought to have made perhaps three-quarters of the campaign pictures of the Army of the Potomac. In 1863, former Brady employees Alexander Gardner, James Gibson, and Timothy O'Sullivan separated from Brady. This was at least partially because they wanted credit and recognition for their own artistic talents; while working for Mathew Brady all of their pictures were marketed under the Brady name, even though many did bear the name of the actual photographer.

After the war, Gardner established his gallery in Washington, D.C. He published a two-volume collection of 100 photographs from the American Civil War, *Gardner's Photographic Sketchbook of the War* (1866), a very expensive product for its day. In 1867, Gardner became the official photographer of the Union Pacific Railroad. As he documented the building of the railroad in Kansas, Gardner photographed Native Americans living in the area. In 1882, he died in Washington, D.C.

Photographic Enlargement

During Robert E. Lee's lifetime, enlargement from a glass-plate negative was possible, but required that a constant amount of sunlight pass evenly through the negative for a long period onto a large sheet of sensitized paper, thereby producing a "solar enlargement." Mathew Brady and Alexander Gardner of New York and Washington were pioneers in this field, making enlargements of various sizes in their solarium even before the Civil War. As early as 1858, Brady was advertising his enlarged photographs, some of which were solar enlargements and some simply made with a camera holding a larger-than-usual "imperial-size" glass-plate negative.

In spite of Brady's work, enlargement of photographs directly from the glass negative was not a practical process until the invention of the constant and reliable illumination provided by the electric light. Catalogs from E. & H. T. Anthony during the 1860s show several solar enlargers for sale. With the exceptions of Mathew Brady, Alexander Gardner, and William Notman (in Canada), solar enlargement was not commonly done during this period, and perhaps not at all in the Confederacy.

One would expect any solar enlargement made from a glass-plate negative to be larger than the standard whole plate ($8\frac{1}{2}$ inches by $6\frac{1}{2}$ inches) simply because it would have been much easier to re-photograph a small image such as a carte de visite with a whole plate in the camera to get a whole plate-sized negative, rather than go through the time-consuming and cumbersome process of passing sunlight through the negative to produce the enlargement. Therefore, generally speaking, all early solar enlargements were images larger than the standard whole-plate size. Any image of Robert E. Lee of a size greater than whole-plate size should be considered a postwar product.

An article in *The Professional and Amateur Photographer* published in 1900 is quite informative:

How best to enlarge the negative has long been an important question. Very early in photography the trouble incident upon the making of large negatives, especially in the wet collodion times, when everything had to be taken to the field, and the work finished on the spot, led men to wish for a method of making small negatives there and enlarging them at home at their leisure. . . . In those days few cared to make landscapes smaller than whole plate, 12" x 10" was common, and although the apparatus for a day's work, after the dry plate came on the scene, was heavy enough to stagger the modern photographer; it was very much less than with the wet collodion [process].[19]

Apparently, many if not most collodion-negative/albumen silver-print photographs taken outside the studio during this period were originally of a size smaller than whole-plate. Many of these were photographically enlarged later.

How Many Views Did Brady Take?

While in Washington in February 1866, in addition to the photographic session with Alexander Gardner, Lee sat for another series

of photographs in Mathew Brady's gallery. Historians, collectors, and dealers have for years assumed that this series of photographs was made in 1869 on Lee's final visit to Washington. In 1986, a scholarly article by Dr. John O'Brien proved this postulation to be incorrect.[20]

For years, only three poses were recognized as products of this sitting. One portrait is a left near profile; another, a near straightforward view, with a slight turn to the right; and the

Large format photograph, a near left profile, made by Mathew Brady of New York and Washington, D.C., in February 1866, which for many years was thought to be one of the only three poses taken at this sitting, labeled "Pose 1" for purposes of this manuscript. Library of Congress

fortable-looking chair that had once been used by Abraham Lincoln, who had presented it to Mathew Brady.[22]

In 1983, another pose taken at this sitting was discovered and published. It shows Lee again positioned obliquely to his left, much as in the "Clock Portrait," but looking very slightly more to the right, enough so that a tiny bit more of his left cheek is visible lateral to his mustache, as well as the lateral corner of his left eye socket. There is also a different

Large format photograph showing a straight forward pose made by Mathew Brady of New York and Washington, D.C., in February 1866, which for many years was thought to be one of the only three poses taken at this sitting, labeled "Pose 2" for purposes of this manuscript. Library of Congress

third, a sitting pose with Lee near a table which held an ornate Victorian clock, the well-known "Clock Portrait." Those who have attempted to pinpoint the time of this photographic session by the time shown on the clock (11:52) will be disappointed to learn that the clock was apparently nonfunctional, as several other Brady photographs show the clock face somewhat askew, exhibiting the same position of the hands.[21] The General sat in a com-

Large format photograph, the "Clock Portrait," made by Mathew Brady of New York and Washington, D.C., in February 1866, which for many years was thought to be one of the only three poses taken at this sitting, labeled "Pose 3" for purposes of this manuscript. National Archives and Records Administration

A Warrior Transformed 95

A pose first recognized in 1983 as part of the February 1866 sitting for Mathew Brady in Washington, D.C., which is labeled for purposes of this manuscript "Pose 4." Shaun Katz

relationship between the right tip of his tie and his lapel. The configuration of his coat at the top of his left shoulder is also different in the two photographs. Additionally, there is a slight dissimilarity in the appearance of the triangles of his white shirt below his tie. These are admittedly minor but real differences, enough to rule out that this "Pose 4" is simply a cropped "Clock Portrait." The example of "Pose 4" shown here is reproduced from the halftone print in the magazine article by Mark Katz, no better copy being available.

The Clock Portrait, "Pose 3," made by Mathew Brady in February 1866, cropped to show head and shoulders for comparison to pose recognized in 1983. National Archives and Records Administration

In 2004, yet another pose, a slight variation of Pose 4, was recognized on a cabinet card bearing Brady's copyright notation. This one shows, among other subtle differences, that the white triangle made by Lee's shirtfront is much more of an elongated isosceles triangle than it is in the other right oblique poses, which show his shirtfront more like an equilateral triangle. The wrinkles in his jacket also do not quite match those in any of the other photographs.[23]

Thus in February 1866, General Lee had a total of five rather than three photographs made at this sitting for Mathew Brady in Washington. The images from Brady's negatives have been copied many times in many formats.

It is an odd fact that some cartes de visite from this sitting for Mathew Brady in 1866 have been found mounted on cards with Brady's 1865 copyright imprint.[24] This has been a source of confusion for many collectors, dealers, and others interested in Robert E. Lee photographs. Perhaps the financially troubled photographer was simply being frugal by using up his supply of outdated card mounts.

After the Brady negatives were removed from storage in the early 1900s by Frederick Meserve, many of the deteriorating glass-plate negatives were used to print photo-graphic copies on more modern gelatin silver photographic paper rather than albumen silver paper. One such copy turned up at an antique shop in Middleburg, Virginia, several years ago.

The most recently recognized pose from the Mathew Brady sitting in Washington, D.C., in February 1866, identified as a separate pose in 2004, and for purposes of this manuscript labeled "Pose 5." Donald A. Hopkins

The Dry-Plate Process

A major step forward for photography came in 1871 with the discovery that gelatin could be used in place of collodion to bind light-sensitive chemicals to a photographic plate as well as photographic paper. This led to the development of the dry-plate process which, with further refinement, allowed for very short exposure times. In addition, dry plates could be developed much more quickly than with any previous technique, and factory-made photographic materials were now possible. Once it was determined that gelatin would bind the light-sensitive silver compounds to paper, it became much easier to prepare printing-out papers in advance and store them until use. Portable darkrooms were no longer necessary. Robert E. Lee had

An example of a photograph of General Lee from Mathew Brady's February 1866, sitting in Washington, D.C., printed out from an original negative several years later as a 7"x 9" dry plate gelatin print. Donald A. Hopkins

died before this process was developed, and therefore there are no original "from life" images of him processed by the dry-plate method.

Notes

Chapter 9: A Warrior Transformed

[1] Henry Alexander White, *Robert E. Lee and the Southern Confederacy*, 1807-1870 (New York, NY, 1897), 31.

[2] Fishwick, *Lee After the War*, 37.

[3] Gorman, "Civil War Richmond" (Richmond, VA, 2008). http://www.mdgorman.com/Written_Accounts/newspaper

[4] Ibid.

[5] Katz, "New Faces," 42-45.

[6] Michael D. Gorman, "Lee the 'Devil' Discovered at Images of War Seminar: Derisive Graffiti Appears in 1865 Brady Photo of Lee," *Center for Civil War Photography Newsletter*, February 2006. http://www.civil-

warphotography.org/index.php/newsletters/117-volume-4-issue-1-february-2006#LeeDevil

7 Lantern Slides are glass plates with images, either painted or photographed, on their surface which, when light is passed through them will project the image on a wall or a screen. The device for generating the light behind the slide was often called a "Magic Lantern."

8 Trent, "Robert E. Lee," vol. 10, 61.

9 Mark D. Katz, *Witness to an Era: The Life and Photographs of Alexander Gardner* (Nashville, TN, 1991), 208.

10 The relatively new copyright laws which applied to photographs protected original work, but not additions to nor embellishments of the original photograph, such as vignetting. A separate copyright could be obtained for any embellishments or additions to the original work, but would not apply to the original material.

11 Katz, "New Faces," 42-45.

12 Hendershott Museum Consultants, catalog description: "This is large imperial sized image made by Alexander Gardner of Washington during the first year of Lee's tenure as President of Washington University. Image 16" x 18". Has Gardner's copyright 1866 on bottom of image." – Little Rock, AR, Gary Hendershott), n.p., n.d. Telephone interview with Gary Hendershott, February 9, 2012.

13 Robert E. Lee to Mrs. Ellen Caskie, March 13, 1866, call no. GLC01433, Gilder Lehrman Institute of American History.

14 Alexander Gardner to Robert E. Lee, April 10, 1866, Leyburn Library, Washington and Lee University.

15 Robert E. Lee to Alexander Gardner, April 25, 1866, Leyburn Library, Washington and Lee University.

16 Adam Plecker, "General Lee on Traveler," *The Confederate Veteran Magazine* (1970) Vol. 30, No. 3, 117.

17 Robert E. Lee to Reverend William C. Greene, April 15, 1867, Leyburn Library, Washington and Lee University.

18 Heritage Collectibles Auctions, "Autograph Letter Signed by Robert E. Lee accompanied by a Signed Carte De Visite of the General in a Confederate Uniform," catalog entry in *June 2007 Civil War Grand Format Auction* (Gettysburg, PA, June 24, 2007), Lot no. 72023.

19 H. Sampson, "Making Enlarged Negatives from Small Ones," *The Professional and Amateur Photographer* (September 1900), vol. 5, 340.

20 John O'Brien, "Brady and Lee, 1866: A History of a Photographic Session," *Military Images*, (March-April 1986), 6-8.

21 Bob Frishman, "Mathew Brady's Clock," *National Association of Watch and Clock Collectors' Bulletin* (October 2002), 605.

22 Roy Meredith, *Mr. Lincoln's Camera Man: Mathew Brady* (New York, 1974), 78-80.

23 Cabinet card in author's collection recognized as another variant after comparing it to "Pose 4." – Donald A. Hopkins, "A New Image of Lee," *North South Trader's Civil War: A Magazine for Collectors & Historians* (Orange, VA, 2004), vol. 30, No. 2, 36-40.

24 Heritage Collectibles Auctions, "Robert E. Lee Carte De Visite," catalog entry in *Manuscripts Grand Format Auction* (New York, NY, December 8-9, 2011), Lot 34057.

CHAPTER 10

THE GENERAL MOUNTS UP

"Just as we went through the four years together."[1]

In the summer of 1866, the Lees visited the mineral spring baths in Rockbridge County, Virginia. These waters seemed to have a salutary effect on Mary Lee's rheumatism, as well as providing the aging General some relief from his own physical complaints.[2]

Adam H. Plecker, a traveling photographer from Lynchburg, primarily a tintypist, employed Michael Miley, who, like himself, was a Confederate veteran. Possibly at Miley's insistence, they decided to make an effort to obtain a photograph of General Lee. Plecker and Miley were pleasantly surprised when Lee readily agreed to be photographed, mounted on his iron-gray horse Traveller. Together the photographers took at least four images of the General and Traveller. In 1922, Adam Plecker wrote a description of this photographic session:

Traveler was then looking his best, about eight years old, a dapple gray, in good condition, well groomed – a very picture himself. It was midsummer, warm, and the flies were very bad, so we had trouble holding him still long enough, as there were no instantaneous pictures made at that time. After several trials I succeeded in getting a satisfactory picture, one of the General mounted and another with him standing by his horse. He then came into the car and I made some small bust photographs of him, one of which Mrs. Lee said was the best picture she had of him to that time. I also made some sittings of his daughters, and later one in the early fall of Mrs. Lee at her residence in Lexington, Virginia.[3]

Besides flies, there was yet another reason that this series of photographs of General Lee and Traveller proved unsatisfactory. The horse had been made nervous and skittish when around strangers by admirers of Lee who at every opportunity plucked hairs from his tail or his mane for souvenirs.[4] The effect of this practice can be seen when we contrast the appearance of the horse's tail in this series of photographs with the healthy bushiness of his tail in photographs made a few months later. This nervousness, along with the unattractive appearance of his ordinarily thick tail and mane and the buzzing and biting of horse flies, brought an end to this photographic session—no doubt to Traveller's relief.

In addition to selling the larger versions of his altered and enhanced pictures (some at least 7 inches by 9 inches), several years later Plecker sold many real photograph postcards bearing these pictures.[5]

Roy Meredith, in his study, stated without citation that Alexander Gardner of Washington had hired Miley to obtain the photograph of Lee on his horse (his only mention of Alexander Gardner throughout the book). This author has not been able to find any basis for this statement, and actually find this scenario very unlikely, as Miley did not even have a studio of his own at the time. Yet

A "real photograph" post card bearing a photograph of General Lee made by Adam H. Plecker and Michael Miley at Rockbridge Baths, Virginia, in the summer of 1866. Valentine Richmond History Center

An example of the paper label Adam Plecker pasted on the message side of his real photograph post cards. Donald A. Hopkins

Gen. R. E. Lee and Traveler, from life 1866.
—By A. H. PLECKER, Soldiers' Home, Richmond, Va.

this myth has been repeated by many students of Lee photographs ever since. It could have originated from a statement found in a massive study of Civil War photographs published in 1912, in which the author stated without reference, "In July of that year Brady, Gardner, and Miley had tried to get a photograph of the general on his horse, but the weather was so hot and the flies accordingly so annoying that the pictures were very poor."[6]

Perhaps a more accurate description of events surrounding this photographic session at Rockbridge Baths was presented in 1941 by Michael Miley's son, Henry. Henry became his father's successor in business. He related:

One of the first pictures of General Lee after he came to Lexington was made at Rockbridge baths. He [Henry's father] and

Plecker went there in a van — a boxcar wagon in which they would travel from place to place and stay as long as business was good. . . . Father took two pictures at Rockbridge Baths — one [of Lee] on his horse and one standing beside it. These were small photographs made on a wet plate and were about 3½" by 4." Plecker had these pictures enlarged and worked up but General Lee did not look natural. Father laughed about Plecker claiming to have made these pictures but as he was working for Plecker the negatives belonged to Plecker, but Father made the sittings himself.[7]

Henry Miley's narrative sheds light on several points. First, nowhere does he mention any business relationship between his father and Alexander Gardner. Second, the size of the "from life" collodion negatives was

One of Adam Plecker's real photograph post cards showing extensive alteration of the photograph which had been taken at Rockbridge Baths, Virginia, during the summer of 1866. Valentine Richmond History Center

A rare unaltered version of one of the photographs of General Lee taken at Rockbridge Baths, Virginia, by Adam Plecker and Michael Miley in the summer of 1866. Washington and Lee University

quarter-plate, as was a tintype which was recognized in 1983 as being from this session. Third, Miley made the two wet-plate negatives while Adam Plecker likely made two tintypes, as this was the latter's specialty. And fourth, any photographs made while Miley was employed by Plecker would be credited to Plecker.

An extremely rare, probably unenhanced, photographic print from this session survives. When compared to his real photograph postcards, this illustrates the extent of Plecker's alteration of this poorly focused photograph for commercial purposes.

One of the tintypes previously mentioned was presented as a new finding by Mark D. Katz in 1983 in a magazine article. This oval-shaped image shows Lee's left rather than his right side, while mounted, and it requires close study to be certain that it is not simply a reversed image of the photograph shown above. The differences are

A rare tintype of Robert E. Lee and his horse Traveller taken by Adam Plecker and Michael Miley at Rockbridge Baths, Virginia, in the summer of 1866.
Shaun Katz

subtle but definite, and include slight variance in the position of the reins in relation to the neck of the horse, the angle of Lee's hat brim, and the position of the horse's rear legs. Traveller is also revolved 180 degrees in relationship to his background. It likewise is a poorly focused photograph.[8] The example shown here is from an old halftone copy, as the original cannot be located.[9]

Research at the Museum of the Confederacy in Richmond turned up evidence of yet another tintype made at this time, probably by Plecker. There is a collodion/albumen copy of this tintype that shows Lee from the right side mounted on his horse. Careful examination shows definite dissimilarities be-

tween this and the other images of Lee mounted on Traveller, including the angle of the reins held by Lee and the space between the horse's tail and his rear leg. An interesting period note in ink accompanies this photograph: "The original of this photograph is a tintype taken for Mrs. Myers and her children at Rockbridge Baths, Va., summer, 1866." Mrs. Myers was the wife of Major Edmund T. D. Myers, an engineering officer who had worked with General Lee during the war improving defenses at Fort Huger and Jamestown.[10] This description of events surrounding the making of this tintype is confirmed by Major Myers' great-great-granddaughter, who happens to work at the Mu-

A collodion/albumen copy of a very rare unpublished tintype of General Lee mounted on his horse Traveller made by Adam Plecker and Michael Miley at Rockbridge Baths, Virginia, during the summer of 1866. Museum of the Confederacy

seum of the Confederacy.[11] Thus, rather than there being only two outdoor photographs made at this time by Plecker and Miley, there were four, two of which were tintypes.

Plecker took his photographs of Lee and Traveller back to his studio in Lynchburg, where he used watercolors and oils to enhance them, then re-photographed them into a

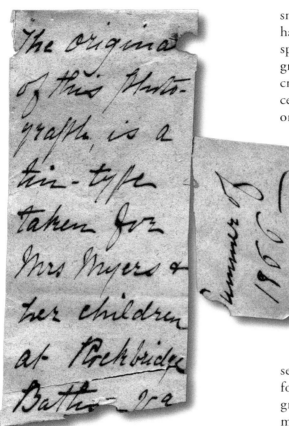

Note accompanying photograph of General Lee and Traveller made at Rockbridge Baths, Virginia, in 1866. Museum of the Confederacy

larger format. In fact, unenhanced versions of these photographs are very rare, the original negatives having been lost or broken long ago. At this point, with rare exception, all images by Plecker and Miley of Lee and Traveller, except the one-of-a kind tintypes, must be considered at least second-generation images. It is unfortunate that most surviving copies of these images are so heavily retouched.

The "Small Bust Photographs" of Lee

As for Plecker's "Small Bust photographs," which he noted as having been taken at this photographic session, one must search through the few Lee photographs found in

small, possibly carte de visite format which have no or only tentative attribution to a specific photographer. Only a few photographs of Robert E. Lee are not definitely credited to a specific photographer or to a certain date. There are yet others which for one reason or another have perhaps been attributed to the wrong photographer.

The images in question should be torso (bust) views in the same suit or altered uniform as shown in Plecker's images of Lee and his horse. At least two photographs seem to meet the proper criteria, one of which is found on a very plain, unadorned card and has been attributed to Michael Miley. Another unattributed and unsigned photograph in the National Archives of Lee in a different pose was evidently taken at the same sitting.

Both pictures show the General in what seems to be the same or very similar uniform coat as seen in the Vannerson photographs made during the war, now lacking military insignia, of course. These two images seem to meet the requirements to be the Small Bust photographs mentioned by Plecker. Plecker was known to use a circular stamp with a date in the center reading "A.H. Plecker's Traveling Gallery" on the back of the paper mats within which he mounted his small tintypes. The original cartes de visite likely had either Plecker's imprint or no imprint whatsoever, since Miley, even if he made the photograph, was an employee of, not a partner with, Plecker. Later copies or altered presentations of these pictures might have either Plecker's or Miley's imprint after the artists had gone their separate ways, or no backmark at all.

A recent auction catalog description of a copy of the more straightforward pose notes the military-style jacket with civilian buttons, and states that there is part of a revenue stamp on the verso, which is "signed" in manuscript by "Kelly" of Lexington, Virginia.[12] The fact that this image originally had an orange revenue stamp establishes that it was sold after the war ended in mid-April 1865 but prior to August 1, 1866, for less than 25 cents. This stamp would have still been in use when Plecker and Miley made their photographs at Rockbridge Baths but not in use when Michael Miley finally opened his gallery later that year. An identical carte de visite mounted on a very plain card, in the collection of the Virginia Historical Society, also has a revenue stamp.[13]

Joseph Kelly

No photographer named Kelly, of Lexington, Virginia, is listed in any of the standard references for nineteenth century Virginia photographers. However, a well-researched study of Rockbridge County artists and artisans reveals that 45-year-old Joseph Kelly was in the Rockbridge County, Virginia, census of 1850 and later in the 1860 census, listed as a cabinetmaker.

According to this account, he was also a photographer who, following the war, "pro-

This example of a carte de visite of a portrait of General Lee, though it has no photographer's imprint, is thought to have been made by Adam Plecker and Michael Miley at Rockbridge Baths, Virginia, in the summer of 1866 and is labeled "Pose 1" for purposes of this manuscript. Dementi Studio

This example of a carte de visite of a portrait of General Lee, though it has no photographer's imprint, is thought to have been made by Adam Plecker and Michael Miley at Rockbridge Baths, Virginia, in the summer of 1866 and is labeled "Pose 2" for purposes of this manuscript. National Archives and Records Administration

duced and distributed" General Lee's cartes de visite and listed himself as a "photographic artist" on Washington Street in Lexington.[14] Oddly enough, the John Boude who was later part of the Boude and Miley photographic partnership also was listed as a cabinetmaker in the 1860 Lexington census.

Did Joseph Kelly "produce" the cartes de visite from life or did he, like many photographers of the time, simply copy and sell someone else's work? From available information, it seems that Joseph Kelly somehow obtained copies of these cartes de visite and "distributed" them, selling at least one copy before August 1866, very shortly after the original was taken. Having at the time no gallery of his own in which to make copies of the photographs, Miley may well have sold prints from the original negatives to Joseph Kelly. It also should be noted that Adam Plecker with his traveling gallery was in Lexington for a few weeks during this same period, and Miley was still associated with him. So it is equally plausible that it was Plecker who sold Kelly some prints, or second-generation negatives made of prints, of the pictures. It is very doubtful that Joseph Kelly actually made these photographs from life, but rather arranged to copy or sell the work of Plecker/Miley.

All known postwar photographs of Lee made after he became president of Washington College (October 1865) and before June 1867 have firm attributions as to the photographer, with the exception of the Small Bust photographs described by Plecker, which heretofore have not been identified. Though somewhat circumstantial, the evidence certainly supports a conclusion that these are the carte de visite-size photographs Adam Plecker/Michael Miley made during the summer of 1866 at Rockbridge Baths.

Adam H. Plecker

Born in 1840 in Rockingham County, Virginia, Adam H. Plecker began his career in 1857 as a traveling photographer, primarily a tintypist. The Civil War intervened and he served as a corporal in the Botetourt Artillery of Virginia. Shortly after the war, he traveled from place to place with his "A.H. Plecker's Traveling Gallery," working as an itinerant photographer along with another young veteran, Michael Miley. Miley evidently was teaching Plecker the collodion/albumen technique that he had just recently learned from John H. Burdette of Staunton, Virginia.

Plecker's boxcar-like wagon held all the equipment for the photographers plus had a small sitting room. Miley's association with Plecker was relatively brief, but he was with him when the images of a mounted Lee and the Small Bust photographs were made at Rockbridge Baths. For a short time after this, Plecker parked his traveling gallery in Lexington where Miley continued to work for him. Plecker is credited with photographs of cadets and also one of burned buildings at the Virginia Military Academy made on September 10, 1866.[15] The nomadic artist waxed poetic in the November 28, 1866, issue of the *Lexington Gazette and Banner*:

> *Gallery on wheels, Ladies recollect*
> *I may be off ere you expect.*
> *Pictures good and prices low*
> *Now's your chance before I go!*[16]

Plecker soon moved on according to schedule, which left Michael Miley without a van or studio in which to continue his work. During the 1870s, Plecker had studios in Salem and Fincastle, Virginia. He opened a studio at the corner of 9th and Main in Lynchburg in 1877, and was for many years the community's leading photographer. He is known best for his collection of portraits of Confederate army officers, many of which are on permanent exhibition at the Valentine Richmond History Center. In 1929, Plecker passed away at the Old Confederate Soldiers' Home in Richmond.

Michael Miley, like many Southerners, virtually idolized Robert E. Lee. He began his efforts to document General Lee in photographs while working for Adam Plecker and continued for the rest of his life. In the fall of 1866, Lee agreed to pose again on his old war-horse, this time for Michael Miley. Miley still had an arrangement to work with Plecker out of his van, which was temporarily located in Lexington. Although Miley later made several other images of Lee, this one became his most well-known. Lee wore his military uni-

form, shorn of all Confederate insignia, along with his cavalry boots, gauntlets, and what appears to be his campaign hat. The original "from life" photograph, as seen in the Museum of the Confederacy in Richmond, shows a man wearing a hat standing on the opposite side of the horse behind Lee, obviously trying to steady the nervous animal. This man's image was very skillfully removed from later copies of the classic photograph by artistically manipulating the original negative or altering a print and rephotographing it.

General Lee had ridden several different horses during the war years, but far and away his favorite was Traveller, a gelding which he acquired in late 1861 in western Virginia. In 1866, he proudly described Traveller's "fine proportions, muscular figure, deep chest,

A rare "from life" large format photograph of General Lee mounted on Traveller taken at Lexington, Virginia, by Michael Miley in the fall of 1866 which shows a man holding the horse steady. Museum of the Confederacy

The more common large format copy of Michael Miley's photograph of General Lee mounted on Traveller taken at Lexington, Virginia, in the fall of 1866 altered to remove evidence of the man holding the horse steady. Donald A. Hopkins

short back, strong haunches, flat legs, small head, broad forehead, delicate ears, quick eye, small feet, and black mane and tail"[17] in a letter to his cousin. Commenting on this photograph, General Lee said, "I do not care for a likeness of myself, but I am gratified to have a good one of Traveller."[18]

In one of the primary sources about Michael Miley's career, 22 pages of oral recollections by his son Henry transcribed in 1941, Henry commented: "General Lee on Traveller was the most salable photograph that Father made of him from direct life. The 1866 photograph, which depicted Lee in uniform for the first time since the end of the

war, was taken in the garden behind the president's house on the Washington College campus."[19]

Any of these photographs of Lee on Traveller must be of a large format and show the figure of a man holding the horse steady to be considered "from life." A. H. Hoen of Baltimore made a widely circulated print of this image after Lee's death to raise money for the Lee monument.

Michael Miley

In the late 1860s, Michael Miley (1841-1918) made some of the best-known images of the aging Robert E. Lee. Among his other accomplishments, he became a pioneer in color photography.

Miley was born in Rockingham County, Virginia. At the age of 19 he joined the Confederate Army, serving in General Thomas J. Jackson's "Stonewall Brigade."

Miley began his photographic career after the war in Staunton, Virginia, where he worked for about a year with John Burdett, becoming adept at the collodion/albumen technique. He introduced this technique to Rockbridge County in 1866 when he worked briefly for Adam Plecker. Exactly when he returned to Lexington is not known, but in November 1866 Miley formed a partnership with Captain John C. Boude of Lexington, Clerk of the Rockbridge County Court; hence the stamp, "Boude and Miley" on his early photographic prints.[20] The photography itself is attributable to Miley alone, since Boude is not known to have had any such knowledge or skill; his occupational experience was primarily as a cabinetmaker.[21]

With Boude's backing, Miley opened a studio and gallery in November 1866 on the corner of Main and Nelson Streets in Lexington, upstairs in the Hopkins Building. Supposedly, Miley sold his first photograph in his new gallery on Christmas Eve 1866. He first advertised in the local newspaper on January 2, 1867, and before long he was able to hire James McCown as an assistant. About April 30, 1870, Michael Miley bought out Boude's interest in the business. His studio was known as The Stonewall Art Gallery, and his images of Robert E. Lee, though many of them were copy photographs, became very popular.

Miley was, for all practical purposes, obsessed with making a photographic record of all things related to the Lee family. He photographed portraits, artifacts, documents, dwellings, furniture, and in addition made copy prints of other photographers' work.

Some of these copy prints he embellished or enhanced, others he did not. Nonetheless, he had no compunction about placing his own imprint on these copies. This practice of Miley's is responsible for the incorrect attribution to Miley of several photographs of General Lee, particularly those made late in his life.

Michael Miley became friends with Lee's sculptor, Edward Valentine. During their interactions with General Lee, Michael Miley and Edward Valentine came to greatly admire each other's professional ability. Valentine had such respect for Miley's talents that after Lee's death he requested that Miley come to Richmond to photograph his latest sculpture of the General.

Most of Michael Miley's negatives of Robert E. Lee were actually copies of other artists' work. Many, but certainly not all, of his negatives related to the Lee family are now at the Virginia Historical Society in Richmond. A detailed listing of these negatives classifies them as follows:

Personal Negatives of Gen. R. E. Lee
    Total Number 57
Statues and Memorials
    Total Number 28
Homes, Office, Personalia
    Total Number 22
Letters and Documents
    Total Number 10
The Lee Family
    Total Number 60
Documents and Personalia
    Total Number 8

The title of a fine biographical study of Miley by Marshall Fishwick, *General Lee's Photographer*, is illustrative of a common perception that Michael Miley made most of Lee's postwar photographs. It will come as a great surprise to some to realize that, of all of Robert E. Lee's postwar "from life" photographs so far recognized (49), Miley can be given unequivocal credit for no more than seven. Even including those made while he worked for Adam Plecker that he claimed to have made, the number would only be nine.

In contrast, other artists, such as Brady (11), D. H. Anderson (5), Plecker (4), Gardner (4), David Ryan (3), Rees (3), Pollock (2), and Tanner and Van Ness (1), as a group can quite confidently be given credit for at least 33 additional postwar photographs of Lee.

About seven other postwar photographic poses of Robert E. Lee remain with no definitive attribution. Most of this latter group are without Miley imprints, and for this and other reasons may well represent the work of other photographic artists.

It is not clear that Michael Miley obtained copyright protection for any of his early photographs. Some of his photographs carry only a simple manuscript notation. But in general, he placed his imprint, often quite elaborately designed, on his work—as well as the work of others.

Notes

Chapter 10: The General Mounts Up

[1] According to Michael Miley, photographer of Lexington, Virginia, General Lee requested that he and his horse be photographed together as they had appeared during the war. – Pendleton, *Traveller*, 27.

[2] Virginia's mineral springs offered the prospect of medical benefits from consumption of the waters and perhaps more appealing to some, a gay social life among the rich and famous. Rockbridge Alum Springs, only about 20 miles from Lexington, was the one visited most frequently by General and Mrs. Lee.

[3] Plecker, "General Lee on Traveller," 117.

[4] Martha Wren Briggs, "The Camera-Shy General," *The United Daughters of the Confederacy Magazine*, March 1994, 18-19.

[5] In the early 1900s, photographic printing-out paper the exact size of a postal card, complete with provisions for a postage stamp, became available. Plecker used some of his old negatives to print his photographs on such cards.

[6] Francis Trevelyan Miller, ed. "Lee on 'Traveller," *The Photographic History of the Civil War* (New York, NY, 1912), vol. 9, 121.

[7] Henry Miley, *Oral Recollections*, 1941 (typescript), Leyburn Library, Washington and Lee University.

[8] Katz, "New Faces," 42-45.

[9] Electronic communication with Shaun Katz, son of the late Mark D. Katz, June 14, 2011.

[10] John M. Carroll, *List of Staff Officers of the Confederate States Army: With a New Introduction by John M. Carroll*, 1861-1865 (Mattituck, NY, 1983), 119.

[11] Personal interview with Ann Drury Wellford, Photograph Archivist, Museum of the Confederacy, Richmond, VA, May 14, 2011.

[12] Cowan's Auctions, "Fine Unpublished, Autographed CDV of Robert E. Lee," catalog entry in *Historic Americana Auction* (Cincinnati, OH, November 16-18, 2005), Lot 1235.

[13] "Carte de visite Photograph, Robert E. Lee in Civilian Dress," Museum and Photograph Record, 2001.2.140, Virginia Historical Society.

[14] Crawford and Lyle, *Rockbridge County Artists*, 208.

[15] Ibid., 48-49.

[16] Marshall Fishwick, *General Lee's Photographer* (Chapel Hill, NC, 1957), 6.

[17] Lee, *Recollections and Letters*, 83.

[18] John William Jones, ed., "Editorial Paragraphs," in *Southern Historical Society Papers* (Richmond, VA, 1977), vol. 2, No. 2, 108.

[19] Crawford and Lyle, *Rockbridge County Artists*, 45-48.

[20] Ibid.

[21] Edwin L. Dooley, Jr., *Transcribed, Corrected, and Annotated, 1860 Census Town of Lexington, Virginia* (Lexington, VA, 2008), n.p. Crawford and Lyle, Rockbridge County Artists, 45-46.

CHAPTER 11

LEE THE ACADEMICIAN

"General Lee was dressed in a plain but elegant suit of gray. His appearance indicated the enjoyment of good health—better, I should say, than when he surrendered his army at Appomattox Court House. . ."[1]

Robert E. Lee, although flattered by a postwar offer to assume the presidency of Washington College, doubted his qualifications as an educator and was apprehensive regarding his physical limitations. His reply to an encouraging letter from Brigadier General W. N. Pendleton, rector of the Episcopal church in Lexington, revealed that the idea of service to young men of the South was a driving force behind his final acceptance of the position.[2] On October 2, 1865, Lee took the oath of office.

Lexington, in the Shenandoah Valley, was still scarred from the effects of the war. The blackened ruins of the Virginia Military Institute rested on a bluff overlooking the Maury River near the desolate and boarded up Washington College. On alternately muddy or dusty Main Street one passed by piles of rubbish and bricks among untidy commercial buildings which varied between one and three stories tall.

Washington College
Staff Composites

The few staff members of Washington College in 1866 are shown in a composite image produced by Michael Miley. Lee, as president, is represented by a tiny image in oval format in the center, surrounded by professors. With his head turned obliquely to the right, Lee is shown wearing a light-colored jacket, possibly his old military jacket, now with plain buttons as required by Federal regulations. An uncommon feature of Lee's wardrobe is his dark, contrasting vest, a feature rarely found in his photographs. He also wears a rather bulky bow tie.

The first composite is made up of pictures of faculty members who were active when Lee became president of the college in October 1865, along with four who joined the staff while the 1866-67 term was in progress. At least four others joined the faculty in 1866 but are not represented in this composite. The composite images are imprinted with the Boude and Miley backmark.

This same image of Lee is found in the center of a later composite of professors of 1868, but it is rarely seen presented as an individual image of the General. An example

A composite photograph in large format showing the Washington College Faculty of 1866/67 with Robert E. Lee as the central figure, made by Michael Miley of Lexington, Virginia, in 1867.
Virginia Military Institute

in carte de visite format of this photograph was found on a website of Civil War generals and brevet generals compiled by Mikel Uriguen.[3] This particular photograph, which has been in the public domain for many years, bears a Miley, Lexington, Virginia, imprint. When compiling this group

A composite photograph in carte de visite format showing the Washington College Faculty of 1867/68 with Robert E. Lee as the central figure, made by Michael Miley of Lexington, Virginia, in 1868. Washington and Lee University

of photographs, Uriguen took this low-resolution copy from a recent auction catalog.

Another postwar photograph attributed to Michael Miley is heavily enhanced; it shows a right profile of Lee in what appears to be the same coat, dark vest, and bulky bow tie. A carte de visite with this image bears the date of April 12, 1868, along with Lee's signature. It appears that these two images were made at the same sitting, using the same

Miley of Lexington was actually made by Charles R. Rees of Richmond. The Virginia Historical Society has an oval black and white photographic print made from an original glass-plate negative of a non-vignetted image from this sitting. The Society makes no attribution as to the original photographer, and the glass-plate negative used to make the print has been lost. This photograph measures 8 inches by 10 inches. The Valentine Richmond

Photograph of Robert E. Lee used for central medallion in the Washington College Faculty composites of 1866-68 taken by Michael Miley of Lexington, Virginia, labeled "Pose 1" for purposes of this manuscript. Mikel Uriguen

more straightforward pose for the school composite for each of the years 1866 and 1868.

Miley put his composites together sometime in 1867 after forming his partnership with John Boude, as most copies bear their imprint.

Charles R. Rees or Michael Miley?

A heavily retouched photograph that Roy Meredith credited in his book to Boude and

Photograph of Robert E. Lee's right profile photograph taken by Michael Miley of Lexington, Virginia, at the same time he made the photograph used for the central medallion in the Washington College faculty composites of 1866-68, labeled "Pose 2" for purposes of this manuscript. Washington and Lee University

History Center describes its copies of these pictures from this photographic sitting as having been made in 1869, with Michael Miley of Lexington being the original photographer.

An upper chest view showing Lee wearing a bulky bow tie and a vest with rounded lapels and sport-ing a watch chain characterize this photographic session. For many years, only two photographic poses have been recognized as showing the General in this combination of attire, and therefore by inference made at the same photographic session. This example of "Pose 2" does not have a photographer's im-

Photograph of Robert E. Lee previously attributed to Michael Miley of Lexington, Virginia, circa 1869, now known to have been made by Charles Rees of Richmond, Virginia, in late 1867, which for purposes of this manuscript is labeled "Pose 2." Mikel Uriguen

Photograph of Robert E. Lee previously attributed to Michael Miley of Lexington, Virginia, circa 1869, now known to have been made by Charles Rees of Richmond, Virginia, in late 1867, which for purposes of this manuscript is labeled "Pose 1." Virginia Historical Society

print. This low-resolution copy was among others compiled from recent auction catalogs.[4]

A deteriorating, large-format example of "Pose 1" from this sitting was recently sold at auction. It is a vignetted view that had been trimmed to a 7½-inch by 5-inch oval, mounted on large, gold-ruled card stock, and imprinted "C. R. Rees and Co. Richmond, Virginia." This photograph has a penciled date on the back, "1867."[5]

Research recently turned up another pose from this sitting which shows a little more of Lee's right profile than "Pose 1." It is a vignetted view that almost obscures the watch chain that passes through the second buttonhole of his vest. It is probably the third pose the photographer made at this sitting, as the bow tie has begun to slip downward on the right.

This third pose is one of the rarest photographs of Robert E. Lee, with only one or perhaps two known examples. There is a very good reason for the scarcity of this image, as evidenced by an affidavit in the archives of the library of the University of Virginia. This legal document is attached to an old 8½-inch by 12½-inch photocopy of the negative of this third pose

made in the Rees gallery. The affidavit, executed in 1957, reads as follows:

> *The attached picture of General Robert E. Lee was made by the firm of Rees & Co. of Richmond Virginia. The negative was taken while Lee was President of Washington*

A virtually unknown photograph of General Lee from a photographic session previously assigned to Michael Miley of Lexington, Virginia, circa 1869, now known to have been made by Charles Rees of Richmond, Virginia, in late 1867, which for purposes of this manuscript is labeled "Pose 3." U.S. Army Heritage and Education Center

College (now Washington and Lee University), and it was one of the last pictures taken of Lee.

Mr. Rees stated that he submitted three negatives to General Lee for his approval. Of the three, Mr. Rees preferred this one from which this picture was subsequently made. General Lee, however, declined this negative and directed Mr. Rees to destroy it because as General Lee stated: "It makes me look more like a prosperous Southern gentleman than a defeated warrior."

Mr. Rees did not obey the General's order but kept the objectionable negative until after Lee's death and made this one picture from it. Later Mr. Rees gave it to his good friend Mr. S. E. Bates, Sr. with the condition that it be always kept in Mr. Bates' family and never published. Mr. Bates kept the picture for about fifty years, and at his death it passed to his son S. E. Bates, Jr. At his death his two daughters, Mrs. Mildred Bates Gwathmey and Mrs. Mary Bates Sydnor inherited the picture and still own it.

The picture hung in the office of E. M. Gwathmey, the husband of Mildred Bates Gwathmey and the president of Converse College in Spartanburg, South Carolina.[6]

The picture no longer hangs in the office at Converse College and its whereabouts are not known.[7]

Carte de visite presentations of both "Pose 1" and "Pose 2" are not infrequently found with imprints from the Rees Gallery on the verso, yet they generally remain attributed to Michael Miley.

During the war, Charles R. Rees marked his cartes de visites with an unembellished imprint "Chs. R. Rees and Co., Photographic Artists, Richmond, Virginia." His brother Edwin worked alongside him, and evidently before the war ended Walter G. R. Frayser joined the establishment. On April 3, 1865, Rees' studio at 145 Main Street was destroyed in the evacuation fire. When the gallery first

Carte de visite with a Rees of Richmond, Virginia, backmark originally attributed to Michael Miley, of Lexington, Virginia. Donald A. Hopkins

reopened for business after this conflagration, it was as "C. R. Rees & Bro.," now that Edwin had become a full partner in the concern. A newspaper report of July 13, 1865, noted that the top story of a building recently completed at the corner of 8th Street and Main Street, fronting on both streets, "will be occupied by Messrs. Rees and Brother, Photographic Artists."[8]

A carte de visite of a Union soldier in occupied Richmond bears a revenue stamp and has the "C. R. Rees and Bro." logo, noting their address as 8th and Main Streets. The revenue stamp confirms that Rees and his brother were in business before August 1, 1866, at their new address. As a result of the changes in the Richmond street numbering system in early 1866, the new gallery's address was redesignated as 911-913 Main Street. The studio was still operating as "Rees & Bro." in early 1867, as shown by a concentric circular date stamp imprint found on a carte de visite with the name of the firm and the date February 26, 1867, but no address. This was a type of stamp previously used to cancel revenue stamps which Rees now, at least in this case, used as his "make do" imprint. At some point in 1867, the partnership expanded once again to include W. G. Frayser. The imprint was again changed, this time to "C. R. Rees and Co." as shown on the verso of a Robert E. Lee photograph from this photographic session which recently sold at auction.[9]

An example of a C. R. Rees and Co. imprint used in mid-1867. Heritage Collectibles Auctions

This is the earliest Rees gallery imprint found on carte de visite examples of either of these poses of Robert E. Lee, and is a backmark probably first used in late 1867 by Rees. The firm's address was 911-913 Main Street, near Ninth, Richmond, Virginia. This seems to have been the first imprint used by the three partners after completing their new business arrangement.

Still later in 1867, the backmark on their cartes de visite was replaced by a detailed engraving of the façade of the new gallery at 911-913 Main Street with all three photographers' names printed underneath. Importantly, the year of the production of the card was imprinted within the logo beneath the photographers' names. During this transition phase between imprints, evidently the company used both the old and the new types of backmark. Cards with the new logo on the reverse were in use by late 1867, as evidenced by a carte de visite of General Beauregard which the Creole signed and dated in early November of that year. This style of backmark that included the date was used by the gallery for several years. There are Robert E. Lee photographs marked with this new imprint, dated 1867 and later, in addition to a few with the old-style imprint.

This evidence indicates that these Robert E. Lee photographs were made after Rees and Company had moved into their new location and at about the time they began using the new dated backmark showing the names of all three artists. Thus, the date of 1869 previously assigned to these photographs is definitely erroneous, as is their attribution to Michael Miley. So when, during the first couple of years after the war ended, might Charles Rees have had an opportunity to photograph General Lee in Richmond?

After arriving in Richmond following the surrender of the Army of Northern Virginia in April 1865, Lee remained there with his family until the end of June, when he moved to a small cottage called Derwent in rural Powhatan County. He and his family lived there until he left for Lexington in mid-September 1865 to

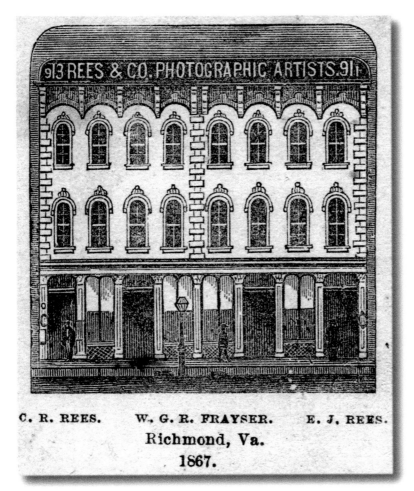

C. R. REES.   W. G. R. FRAYSER.   E. J. REES.
Richmond, Va.
1867.

An example of the imprint found on the verso of Rees and Company cartes de visites beginning in late 1867. Donald A. Hopkins

In January 1866, Lee made a difficult trip back to Richmond from Lexington to appeal to the General Assembly of Virginia for support for Washington College. There is no record indicating that he took time for a photographic session during this visit. He remained there for a week, during which he avoided social situations and publicity as much as possible. If Lee had his picture taken by Rees during this visit, the carte de visite would not yet have had a backmark with Rees' 911-913 Main Street address. Also, photographs sold during this early postwar period required revenue stamps until August 1866. Of the few cartes de visite of these Lee photographs available for examination, none have evidence of such a stamp, and all have the 911-913 Main Street address which began to appear on the Rees gallery card mounts sometime in 1867.

In late November 1867, Lee made another visit to Richmond. His son Rooney was to be married in nearby Petersburg. In addition,

assume the presidency of Washington College. Had the General been inclined to sit for more photographs before he left the city, he could not have posed for Charles Rees, because Rees' gallery was not yet operational.

Lee had been subpoenaed as a witness in the trial of Jefferson Davis for treason, to be held in Richmond at about the same time. During this visit, he purchased a new broadcloth suit in Richmond for the wedding.[10] Lee arrived at Richmond on the evening of the 25th of November. He participated in legal matters on the morning of November 26th, leaving Richmond for Petersburg during the afternoon of the following day. He likely wore his newly purchased suit when he sat for photographs in Rees' gallery. The only opportunity Lee had to buy a new suit was the afternoon of the 26th or the morning of the 27th, after which he might have had his photograph made before leaving for Petersburg. However he also could have sat for the photographs when he passed back through Richmond on his way home. There were several opportunities during this visit, which extended from November 25th until December 6th, for the General, who was now enjoying socializing, to have his photograph taken by Rees. After General Lee posed for these pictures for Rees, the photographer evidently used leftover cards with his recently outdated imprint to mount a few of the prints.

Based on analysis of all the currently available information, it is apparent that these photographs were made in late November or early December 1867 by Charles Rees or one of his associates at the Rees gallery in Richmond.

Charles R. Rees

Having moved from New York, Charles R. Rees was well established as a photographer in Richmond before the outbreak of the Civil War. In 1860, he moved into Pratt's impressive studio at 143 Main Street. In addition to his photographs, Rees sold a variety of cases for daguerreotypes and ambrotypes. Later in December 1861, he offered other photographic materials and supplies.

Charles' brother Edwin J. Rees worked with him during this period, and together they made several outdoor photographs of Richmond scenes during the war. Walter G.

R. Frayser was listed as an "artist" with the firm. In mid-1863, they were among the first in Virginia to offer their own cartes de visite of Confederate officials and military officers.[11] Their gallery was one of the most active in Richmond during the war, but business evidently began to decline during its last year. When the Rees' establishment burned during the evacuation fire, most of their negatives were destroyed.

Sometime prior to the end of August 1866, the firm reopened as "C. R. Rees & Bro.," with Edwin now a full partner. Frayser soon became a partner in the firm, at which time they restyled themselves "C. R. Rees & Company." The partnership dissolved in 1871 when Frayser opened his own business and Edwin Rees moved to Petersburg.

Robert E. Lee and Jefferson Davis—Really?

One of Jefferson Davis' biographers, Felicity Allen, recorded that General Lee and President Davis had their photographs taken together in Richmond on November 25, 1867, after Davis' trial for treason was again postponed. She relates the following:

Davis was staying at the home of his attorney, Judge Ould. General Lee came to see him there. Someone took their picture together, seated at a marble top table, looking solemn, as all before the camera in those days (except Judah Benjamin). Lee had his full grizzled beard; Davis had shaved his prison one down to chin whiskers. Lee was in Richmond to testify before the grand jury preparing a fresh indictment against Davis.[12]

Caution is warranted before interpreting Mrs. Allen's account too literally. She is evidently describing a "drawing" or print, derived from photographs, rather than an actual photograph.[13] The print appeared in a memorial tribute to Jefferson Davis, first published in 1890, and appears as she described it. The introduction to the original 1890 Memorial volume reads in part:

The publishers have, at great expense, and by exercising unusual care and patience, succeeded in securing a large number of beautiful and attractive illustrations for the Davis Memorial Volume, many of which are of rare historical value. We are greatly indebted to W. L. Sheppard whose intimate acquaintance and association with many of the characters and scenes presented in the book enabled him to not only draw for us many striking and in-

teresting pictures, but to make suggestions that were exceedingly helpful to other artists engaged in preparing illustrations for this book. Mr. W. W. Davies, of the Lee Gallery, Richmond, Virginia, also places us under everlasting obligations to him by furnishing many photographs taken during and soon after the war. . . . The originals of these and other photographs used in illustrating this book are now in the possession of Mr. Davies of Lee Gallery. . . .[14]

Careful reading of this passage shows that the "striking and interesting" drawings were simply derived from photographs, the negatives

First meeting of President DAVIS and General LEE after the close of the war, at the residence of Hon. R. Ould, Richmond, November 25, 1867.

A detailed print based on photographs showing Robert E. Lee and Jefferson Davis together for the last time as found in the *Davis Memorial Volume.* Donald A. Hopkins

of which were, in 1890, owned by William W. Davies. For this and other reasons, it seems that this illustration in the Memorial Volume is simply a rendering of "what might have been," by using actual photographs of the subjects as models for the print artists. This was a common practice at the time.

Examination of General Lee's travel itinerary for November 25, 1867, shows that he reached Richmond that afternoon and went to the Exchange Hotel. Only after supper and a round of visits to friends did he appear at Judge Ould's home where Jefferson Davis was staying. There simply could not have been enough daylight (if any) to allow for a photographic session. Neither Lee nor Davis nor anyone who actually witnessed this occasion left any record of what they said or did, and none mentioned photographs being taken.

This very skillfully executed print showing the two old Confederates together is interesting in that the illustration of Jefferson Davis is in detail very much like a photograph of him recently identified by a private collector. This vignetted, carte de visite-size image of Davis wearing an oddly asymmetrical tie has a William W. Davies, Lee Gallery, Richmond, Virginia, backmark. It was almost certainly the model for Jefferson Davis' figure for the print.

A photograph of President Davis in another private collection, showing him posed standing in a studio, is obviously from the same sitting. This one, however, has a D. H. Anderson copyright notation dated July 1867, which firmly establishes that these photographs of Davis were made at least five months before

An example of the carte de visite used as a model for the print showing Robert E. Lee and Jefferson Davis together. Douglas York

Lee and Davis met at Judge Ould's home. The only opportunity that Anderson might have had to photograph Davis in Richmond was during a very brief period in mid-May after Davis' release from prison on bond but before he left Richmond for New York and Canada. However, there is no record that he did so.[15]

As the Davieses were not in the photography business in 1867, they could not have made any photograph of Lee and Davis together at this time. It was not until two years later that they opened their photography enterprise at Lee Gallery.

A photograph of General Lee was found alongside this photograph of Davis in the same old album. Both are mounted on identical red-ruled cards and have identical Lee Gallery backmarks. Another pose of General Lee, obviously taken at the same sitting, when laterally reversed, strikingly resembles the representation of him in the print seated

across the table from Davis. This cabinet card has a D. H. Anderson, Richmond, imprint.

It seems quite likely that this photograph of General Lee was among those prints and negatives "taken during and shortly after the war" that Davies had acquired from other photographers such as Anderson and Vannerson. A very similar image, photographed from a slightly different angle and heavily enhanced, is credited to Michael Miley in 1868 by Miley's biographer, Marshall Fishwick, but there seems

Verso of a cartes de visite of Robert E. Lee which shows William Davies' Lee Gallery backmark as used in the early 1870s. Douglas York

Carte de visite copy of a photograph of Robert E. Lee with a William W. Davies, Lee Gallery backmark. Labeled "Pose 1" for use in this manuscript. Douglas York

An example of a cabinet card size photograph of Robert E. Lee with imprint of D. H. Anderson, Richmond, Virginia, likely used as model for a print showing Lee seated across the table from Jefferson Davis, labeled "Pose 2" for use in this manuscript. Gilder Lehrman Institute of American History

Richmond photographers—Vannerson, Anderson, or, less likely, Davies—would have had an opportunity to photograph General Lee before his death on October 12, 1870. These Lee photographs, which were evidently used as a model for the print in the Davis memorial volume in 1890, were most likely made by D. H. Anderson or someone working for him, such as Julian Vannerson.

A photograph heretofore attributed to Michael Miley of Lexington, Virginia, circa 1858, labeled "Pose 3" for use in this manuscript. Dementi Studio

to be little evidence to support an attribution of the original photograph to Michael Miley.[16] It is apparently a third pose taken at this same photographic sitting.

At least one of these poses is found with a Lee Gallery (operated by the Davies family) backmark, and another is found with D. H. Anderson's imprint. The Davieses bought out Vannerson's Richmond studio, apparently including his negatives, in about 1869, and remained in the photography business until 1891. For the first ten years of their operation, D. H. Anderson was a competitor in business in Richmond before he sold out to George Cook in April 1880. Any one of these three

Notes
Chapter 11: Lee the Academician

[1] Franklin L. Riley, upon observing the swearing-in ceremonies of Lee as president of Washington College. – Lattimore, Lee, 84.

[2] Freeman, *Lee*, vol. 4, 216.

[3] Mikel Uriguen, "Civil War Generals in Black and White." http://www.generalsandbrevets.com/sgl/leere11.htm

[4] Ibid.

[5] Cowan's Auctions, "Scarce Unpublished 1867 Rees Photograph of Robert E. Lee," catalog entry in *Historic Americana Auction* (Cincinnati, OH, Dec. 4-5, 2008), Lot 124.

[6] "Explanatory Statement concerning Rees & Co. Photograph of Robert E. Lee, 1956," Accession #5457, University of Virginia Library, Charlottesville, VA.

[7] Telephone interview with Dr. Jeffrey Willis, Director of Archives and Special Collections, Converse College, Spartanburg, SC, March 16, 2012.

[8] "Building in the Burnt District of Richmond," *The Norfolk Post*, July 13, 1865.

[9] Heritage Collectibles Auctions, "Robert E. Lee Carte de Visite signed R. E. Lee," catalog entry in 2008 *November Signature Civil War Auction* (Dallas, TX, 2008), Lot No. 57125.

[10] Freeman, *Lee*, vol. 4, 334.

[11] Ruggles, *Photography in Virginia*, 49.

[12] Felicity Allen, *Jefferson Davis, Unconquerable Heart* (Columbia, MO, 1999), 493.

[13] John William Jones, *The Davis Memorial Volume: or, Our Dead President, Jefferson Davis and the World's Tribute to his Memory* (Richmond, VA, 1890), 391.

[14] Ibid, front matter.

[15] Jefferson Davis had several photographs made by William Notman of Montreal while in Canada. This photograph may well be a Notman product, for which D. H. Anderson somehow obtained a United States copyright in July 1867.

[16] Fishwick, *General Lee's Photographer*, 40.

CHAPTER 12

A CHAMPION FOR UNITY, BOTH NORTH AND SOUTH

"I have seen all the great men of our times, except Mr. Lincoln, and I have no hesitation in saying that Robert E. Lee was incomparably the greatest looking of them all."[1]

General Lee continued to favor his admirers from both North and South by inscribing photographs they sent to Lexington for his signature. A letter to "Miss Lella" dated April 12, 1868, found among the Robert E. Lee Papers at Washington and Lee University illustrates the General's quaint sense of humor. He wrote, "In gathering up the pictures from my disordered table yesterday, where they had been scattered to dry, one was overlooked. I know you will wonder at the amount of honesty required to part with such a specimen of art, but I assure you in all truth that I have no desire to retain it, & am entitled to no credit in returning it which I now do."[2]

Back to Washington via Baltimore

According to correspondence from Mrs. Lee to General Lee's older brother, Carter Lee, on April 21, 1869, her husband left for Baltimore, arriving there the following evening after a journey of less than two days.[3] He made this trip after having been ill for several days, in order to attend to business regarding a railroad he deemed important to the Valley of Virginia. During this ten-day trip he did have enough time away from business meetings to visit relatives and friends, and presumably to have

his photograph taken if he chose to do so, which apparently he did. Two uncommon cartes de visite showing Lee for the first time wearing a necktie are each blind-stamped by Pollock (of Baltimore).

These collodion/albumen photographs show a careworn and chronically ill older man. A copy of this photograph signed by the General has a penciled note on the back stating that Lee signed it in September 1869, establishing the photo was made before that date. This photograph was likely taken during Lee's short visit to Baltimore because we know he did not return there for his next and final visit until 1870. For many years it was

listed at 147 Lexington Street; a year later, he had relocated to 155 Baltimore Street, where he remained until 1867. At the time he made Lee's photograph, his salon was at 44 Lexington Street, where he operated his gallery until 1886. During one period he produced "5500 likenesses annually." He periodically received high praise in the local newspapers.[4]

A carte de visite of Robert E. Lee made by Henry Pollock of Baltimore, Maryland, in April of 1869, for purposes of this manuscript labeled "Pose 1." Donald A. Hopkins

thought that only a single photograph was taken during the 1869 sitting, but a second and slightly different pose was recently located in the collection of the Museum of the Confederacy in Richmond.

Henry Pollock

Henry Pollock was born in Washington, D.C., and by 1848 was a well-respected daguerreotypist, ambrotypist, and photographer of Baltimore. In 1849, his studio was

A cabinet card of Robert E. Lee made by Henry Pollock of Baltimore, Maryland, in April of 1869, for purposes of this manuscript labeled "Pose 2." Museum of the Confederacy

The "Smiling Picture"

Lee sat for an interesting portrait by Michael Miley in Lexington, as evidenced by a carte de visite of the resulting image with Lee's signature and Miley's imprint.

Heretofore only one photograph has been attributed to this sitting, a torso view with Lee facing obliquely to the right. Lee's stylish wardrobe, including an extremely light-col-

A portrait known as Lee's "Smiling Picture" which was taken by Michael Miley of Lexington Virginia, circa mid-late 1869, bearing imprint of Boude and Miley, labeled "Pose 1" for purposes of this manuscript. Donald A. Hopkins

ored vest or waistcoat, sets this image apart. Oddly enough, the left end of his tie is quite shaggy-looking when seen in enlargement. His waistcoat is hardly visible as a very narrow line following down inside the right lapel of his dark coat in the unaltered version. It is also noticeable in the more common heavily enhanced version. This view presents the nearest thing to a smile noted in any of the General's postwar photographs; it is indeed sometimes called Lee's "Smiling Picture."

Most authorities have dated this photographic session as occurring in 1869 or 1870. However, the archives at Washington and Lee University hold a carte de visite version of this image with a period manuscript note on the back, along with Miley's imprint, indicating that it was signed on October 3, 1867. This note seems to be an inaccuracy resulting from a faulty memory, perhaps added later. General Lee sent a copy of this same photograph to the librarian at the Peabody Institute along with a letter in his hand dated September 25, 1869. He stated in the letter that it was "the last that has been taken."[5] This establishes with

General Lee's "Smiling Picture" cropped and enlarged to show details of the "Shaggy Tie." Donald A. Hopkins

and September 1869: one with Rees of Richmond in very late 1867 and one with Pollock of Baltimore in April 1869. This "Smiling Picture" was made by Michael Miley between April 1869 and September 1869.

There is another photograph, often cited as being made around January 10, 1870, which actually seems to have resulted from the same photographic session as the "Smiling Picture." It too is a very heavily enhanced Michael Miley product, shown as "Pose 2." This view, with Lee facing obliquely to the left, shows more of the General's torso and exposes more of his white shirt and the characteristic, very light-colored waistcoat. Details of Lee's hair and beard (now almost white), tie, and shirt collar are identical in these two photographs.

An additional heavily retouched pose, labeled "Pose 2" for purposes of this manuscript, which was just recently recognized as having been made at the same sitting as Lee's "Smiling Picture" by Michael Miley of Lexington, Virginia, circa mid-late 1869. Dementi Studio

certainty that this photograph was made at a sitting that took place before September 1869. Had it been made before October 1867, it certainly would not have been "the last that has been taken," as stated in the letter, because Lee had two well-documented photographic sittings between October 1867

A print made from one of Michael Miley's 8-inch by 10-inch glass-plate negatives of this retouched right oblique view bears an old manuscript attestation from Michael Miley's son, Henry: "Authentic unknown original photograph of General Robert E. Lee. This print was made from the original negative before which General Lee sat for my father in 1869. Known to be his last photograph in life. . . . Attested to by H. M. Miley."[6] Henry Miley obviously attested to information gained from someone else, likely his father, as he was not yet born in 1869. Enhanced and retouched versions of these two photographs became very popular. Even Adam Plecker sold a beautifully mounted, enhanced, and vignetted copy.

The erroneous conclusion that this was Lee's last photographic session was possibly reinforced by a letter Lee wrote to an admirer. On January 10, 1870, Lee signed a carte de visite of the "Smiling Picture" and enclosed it in a letter, in which he stated, "It is the last that has been taken and is the only kind I have. . . ." This letter and the date on the carte de visite could be used to corroborate Henry Miley's statement that this was the last photograph taken of Lee up to that time, but the General definitely had later photographs made prior to his death. For instance, he participated in group photographs in the early fall of 1869, and others even later. Whether the group pictures were made before or after the "Smiling Picture" remain unclear.

The Gathering at White Sulphur Springs

In August 1869, General Lee made a trip for his health to White Sulphur Springs in West Virginia, his third annual trip.[7] While there he was joined by several ex-Confederate officers and other prominent male citizens from both the North and the South. In the relaxed atmosphere of "The White," these notables held discussions aimed at promoting a sense of unity throughout the country, which was still quite fragmented politically, both north and south of the Mason-Dixon line. Late one afternoon, they gathered for group photographs.

The participants were instructed by the photographers to be, on August 11, 1869, at 4:00 p.m., at the head of Baltimore Row, Cottage #9, and "if convenient, please be punctual."[8] Other than Lee, the best-known Confederates in the group included Generals P. G. T. Beauregard, John B. Magruder, James Conner, and Henry A. Wise. Union Generals Geary and Wallace were also in the photograph, as were the philanthropists George Peabody and W. W. Corcoran. In spite of a great deal of study over the years, the sitters for these photographs were not correctly identified until 1935.[9] Over the years, three different views of this group have been recognized. The photographs were originally made in whole-plate size by D. H. Anderson and G. G. Johnson. Lee is seen to shift his position slightly in each one, most obvious in the changing of positions of his hat. He is rather fashionable, in a shirt with curved collar tabs and a necktie, although his chronic illness is quite apparent. He is privileged to sit in a captain's chair while the others stand or sit on simple, armless side chairs.

While gathering material for this manuscript, two additional variations of this famous photograph were identified, one in a private collection and another in an auction catalog of the past few years. With no access to the original photograph, the latter can only be represented here by the low-resolution illustrations taken from the auction catalog. These five photographs are presented alongside each other for the first time. In one variation, dapper General James Connor of South Carolina is shown to have shifted his position to stand on the opposite end of the back row. (The poses are labeled numerically for presentation in this manuscript, not necessarily in the order in which they were made.)

An example of one of several group portraits which included General Lee made at White Sulphur Springs, West Virginia, in August 1869, by D. H. Anderson and G. G. Johnson, for purposes of this manuscript labeled "Pose 1." Washington and Lee University

An example of one of several group portraits which included General Lee made at White Sulphur Springs, West Virginia, in August 1869, by D. H. Anderson and G. G. Johnson, for purposes of this manuscript labeled "Pose 2." Library of Virginia

An example of one of several group portraits which included General Lee made at White Sulphur Springs, West Virginia, in August 1869, by D. H. Anderson and G. G. Johnson, for purposes of this manuscript labeled "Pose 3."
Seth McCormick-Goodhart

An example of one of several group portraits which included General Lee made at White Sulphur Springs, West Virginia, in August 1869, by D. H. Anderson and G. G. Johnson, for purposes of this manuscript labeled "Pose 4."
Virginia Historical Society

An example of one of several group portraits which included General Lee made at White Sulphur Springs, West Virginia, in August 1869, by D. H. Anderson and G. G. Johnson, for purposes of this manuscript labeled "Pose 5." Heritage Collectibles Auctions

A cropped version of the large group image that shows only General Lee, George Peabody, and William W. Corcoran (labeled as the second pose) has erroneously been considered by some to be a separate photograph.[10]

David H. Anderson

D. H. Anderson was originally from New York. After working in various locations in the West and South, he settled in Richmond, Virginia, in 1866, and remained there until about 1880, when he sold out to George Cook.[11] In 1866, an ad in the *Daily Dispatch* announced that "Anderson Art Palace" had recently employed Mr. M. J. Powers, who had been Vannerson's "principal operator for the past year." Anderson, with his large staff, became well-known for making group portraits as well as very fine salt prints. At some point he opened a branch gallery in Norfolk.

At the time these photographs were made at White Sulphur Springs, his primary address was 1311 Main Street, Richmond, although he may have had a studio at White Sulphur Springs at least during the tourist season. At some point a photographer named Addison A. Knox worked with him at Norfolk and at White Sulphur Springs.[12] No matter at which of his branch operations a photograph was made, Anderson evidently imprinted it with his Richmond address.

In 1875, Anderson was working with Julian Vannerson in both Norfolk and Richmond, but it is unclear exactly when Anderson branched out to the Norfolk area. The Norfolk and Portsmouth Business Directory of 1875-1876 shows that he operated a studio at 208 and 210 Main Street, Norfolk, while maintaining his home in Richmond.[13] By 1877, he had moved his Richmond operation to Rees' old location at 913 Main Street. Anderson sold his business, including his negatives, to George Cook in April 1880, at which time he returned to New York.

Little is known of G. G. Johnson. A very neat manuscript inscription appears on the back of one of the oversized cards bearing this group photograph: "Anderson & Johnson, White Sulphur Springs, Virginia." This card also bears the imprint of "D. H. Anderson, 1311 Main Street, Richmond, Va." On August 20, 1869, a Richmond newspaper reporting on the group photograph recorded that it was made by "Anderson and Johnson of Anderson's Richmond photographic establishment."[14] It seems that Anderson brought supplies including cards for mounting photographs from Richmond for use in a branch operation at White Sulphur Springs, but he might not have bought enough oversized cards for mounting these group photographs to satisfy the demands of the genteel crowd at "The White." A copy of one variation of this photograph is mounted on an oversized board which, on its verso, has a faded gilt oval border with "Western Lunatic Asylum Staunton, Virginia" and "photographed by Clinedinst." Barnett M. Clinedinst operated a studio in Staunton, Virginia, from shortly after the Civil War

until about 1880. Apparently he photographed the infamous Western Lunatic Asylum in Staunton, and this card mount had been prepared for that picture. Somehow, perhaps by purchase, Anderson may have obtained a supply of Clinedinst's large-size cards for his own use, or Clinedinst might have obtained either a negative or print of this poorly focused photograph and marketed it himself.[15]

A Trip to the South

During the spring of 1870, General Lee made a southward tour in the company of his daughter Agnes. He sought relief from his chronic heart and pulmonary complaints in a warmer climate. On April 2, 1870, Lee joined several of his old comrades in Savannah who had come to pay their respects during a dinner party at Andrew Low's home. General Joseph E. Johnston was among the guests. This was the first time these two Southern generals had seen each other since the war.

During his eleven-day stay in Savannah, Lee was convinced by members of "The Ladies Memorial Association," which was raising funds for a Confederate memorial, to have his photograph made alongside General Johnston.[16] This sitting at David Ryan's gallery in downtown Savannah produced three images of the two old West

One of three poses of Generals Lee and Johnston together in Savannah in April 1870, as photographed by David J. Ryan of Ryan's Gallery of Savannah, Georgia, labeled "Pose 1" for purposes of this manuscript. Museum of the Confederacy

David J. Ryan

In 1860, David Ryan was listed in a Charleston, South Carolina, business directory, on King Street working with E. Gardner. He remained in Charleston at least until 1861 before relocating to Savannah.[17] According to his imprint, Ryan's Photographic Gallery was located at the corner of Congress and Whitaker Streets, "Over Mallon & Frierson's Store" in Savannah, Georgia. His backmark has been found on cartes de visite of Union soldiers in occupied Savannah. He also sold stereographic views as well as copies of other Robert E. Lee photographs. Ryan died in 1923.

One of three poses of Generals Lee and Johnston together in Savannah in April 1870, as photographed by David J. Ryan of Ryan's Gallery of Savannah, Georgia, labeled "Pose 2" for purposes of this manuscript. Library of Congress

Point classmates, each 63 years of age, facing each other across a small table, two with Lee seated on the right and one with him on the left. For some reason, Roy Meredith and other students of Lee photographs have generally assigned only two images to this sitting, but Ryan clearly made three different photographs. Of the two poses with Lee on the right side of the table, only one shows an inkwell on the table. "Pose 3" is here represented by a high-resolution copy of an old halftone copy of a photograph which has been in the public domain for years, an original photograph not being available.

One of three poses of Generals Lee and Johnston together in Savannah in April 1870, as photographed by David J. Ryan of Ryan's Gallery of Savannah, Georgia, labeled "Pose 3" for purposes of this manuscript. Donald A. Hopkins

Notes

Chapter 12: A Champion for Unity, Both North and South

[1] Wise, *End of an Era*, 342.

[2] Robert E. Lee to "Miss Lella," April 12, 1868, in Robert E. Lee Papers, Leyburn Library, Washington and Lee University.

[3] "To my dear brother Carter, April 21, [1869]," letter from Mary Custis Lee to Charles Carter Lee, Leyburn Library, Washington and Lee University.

[4] Craig, "Henry Pollock" in *Craig's Daguerreian Registry*.

[5] "Mr. Peabody and His Friends" [scrapbook], George Peabody Papers, Peabody Institute Library Papers, Peabody, Maine.

[6] "Lee, Robert E., Probably the Last Photograph," Negative No. 5023-A'23, Dementi Studio Archives, Richmond, Virginia.

[7] The mineral springs that the Lees seemed to enjoy most was the elaborate and expansive White Sulphur Springs near Greenbrier, West Virginia.

[8] Cowan's Auctions, "Robert E. Lee and Confederate Generals at White Sulphur Springs, WV, Plus," catalog entry in *American History Including the Civil War* (Cincinnati, OH, June 23, 2011), Lot 43.

[9] "Nation's Most Famous Historical Photograph Identified," *The Lexington Gazette* (Lexington, VA, August 21, 1935).

[10] Charles William Dabney, *Universal Education in the South* (Chapel Hill, NC, 1936), vol. 1, 82.

[11] Craig, "D. H. Anderson," in *Craig's Daguerreian Registry*.

[12] T. Dixon Tennant, "Editor's Table," *Wilson's Photographic Magazine* (1909), vol. 46, 144.

[13] Norfolk and Portsmouth Business Directory, 1875-76. http://www.npl.lib.va.us/smrt/directories/1875-1876NorfPort

[14] Untitled article, *Richmond Daily Whig*, August 20, 1869, p. 3, c. 2. http://bfparker.blog.co.uk/2011/10/18/14-of-14-george-peabody-1795-1869-a-z-handbook-of-the-massachusetts-born-merchant-in-the-south-london-based-banker-and-philanthropist-s-life-infl-12030377/

[15] Telephone communication with Seth McCormick-Goodhart, Lexington, VA, April 13, 2012.

[16] James G. Barber, ed., *Faces of Discord: The Civil War Era at the National Portrait Gallery* (New York, NY, 2006), 266-267.

[17] Teal, *Partners with the Sun*, 96.

CHAPTER 13

THE FINAL YEARS

"And I may add that an artist, above all other men, is quick to observe the faintest suggestion of posing; the slightest indication of a movement or expression which smacks of vanity he is sure to detect."[1]

The author recognizes that his postulates regarding the next few images presented in this chronicle of Robert E. Lee photographs are subject to challenge. There is simply very little primary information available regarding these pictures. Such information that is available was diligently sought out and utilized in this presentation. Most material relating to these few poses of the General is found entangled in a confusing web of fact and speculation in earlier works on the subject. The writer is confident that in addition to evidence submitted here, a careful forensic photographic analysis of Alexander Gardner's copyrighted near right profile pose will bear out that it was used by Michael Miley in a later presentation. One cannot refute that the identical hairline, jawline, eyelash line, shape of nostrils, and iris and pupillary position are the same in each version. The standing poses presented here as having been made as models for Edward Valentine's sculpture may not have been all of the poses taken during this sitting; some may yet be discovered or at least not yet connected to this photographic session.

Robert E. Lee's Last Photograph—or Not?

Uncertainty has clouded the issue of which of Robert E. Lee's photographs was the last taken prior to his death in October 1870. Two or three different photographs of the old General have throughout the years been given the exalted title of "the last photograph of Robert E. Lee from life." Most authorities have accepted that the following photograph, the original of which was long attributed to Miley, was made by him before mid-June 1870, and was Lee's final photograph. Lee signed several collodion/albumen carte de visites of this photograph, including one with a presentation date of June 14, 1870, which he presented to Edward Valentine.

However, the attribution of this photograph to Michael Miley with a date of 1870, despite being the commonly held belief, is definitely erroneous. In addition, it could not have been Robert E. Lee's last photograph, since the original was actually made in large format in 1866 by Alexander Gardner, as discussed earlier. In Miley's version, the General's wardrobe and several other features of the photograph are exactly the same as seen in Alexander Gardner's work. Michael Miley

A photographic copy produced by Michael Miley of Lexington, Virginia, before June 14, 1870, thought by many to be "General Robert E. Lee's last photograph from life." Dementi Studio.

seems to have copied every photograph of Robert E. Lee he could obtain, sometimes changing the picture's presentation or enhancing the photograph before applying his own imprint. Furthermore, Miley produced his altered version before buying out John Boudes' interest in their partnership in April

1870, as signed copies have been noted with the Boude and Miley imprint.

An even-further-enhanced gelatin silver version of this photograph has a very interesting history. Old, early twentieth century, typed information, albeit unsigned, that accompanies a large-format print of Miley's en-

"*Last Photograph General Robert E. Lee.*"   JAKE FISHER ©

Michael Miley's enhanced, gelatin silver copy of a photograph of Robert E. Lee made by Alexander Gardner in 1866, re-discovered and copyrighted by Jake Fisher, circa 1917. Donald A. Hopkins

hanced version of Alexander Gardner's photograph is revealing:

This photograph was taken by M. Miley at Lexington about twenty days before General Lee was stricken on September 28, his death following on October 12, 1870. It is his last photograph. One print was made from the plate and the print loaned to Miss Mary Lee, the General's daughter, from which she said she had a cut made. Then the plate was broken, no other print having been made. The one print became misplaced. Later Miley and General Custis Lee had a furious quarrel, the issue being whether Miley had loaned the one print to Miss Mary, which the General denied, or whether Miss Mary had borrowed the photograph and failed to return it, as Miley asserted. The issue was never settled until about 1917 (after the death of both Miley and Custis Lee) when Paul M. Penick, the treasurer of Washington & Lee, found the print, on the back of which were notations regarding the cut, and which was wrapped in cloth. It had evidently been used for the cut, then the print was stored with other papers and forgotten. Judge Jake Fisher, learning of the discovery, attempted to secure the print from Mr. Penick, who refused the request, until his father, Reverend Penick, prevailed upon him to let the Judge have it. Judge Fisher then copyrighted it and had copies made for some of his friends. This photograph is unique, not only in that it is from the sole copy of the last picture taken, but also in that it is regarded as the best likeness of the General.[2]

Apparently Michael Miley copied the 1866 Alexander Gardner photograph and altered and enhanced it in 1870, perhaps so that his presentation would not infringe upon the Gardner copyright. This altered version produced by Miley is the photograph which Judge Fisher considered the last photograph of Lee, even though the original had been made by Alexander Gardner in 1866. Miley likely did produce his markedly altered and enhanced copies during the final year of Robert E. Lee's life, but this was certainly not a "from life" photograph.

The last well-documented photographic session that Robert E. Lee sat (or stood) for was in June 1870, for Michael Miley, under the guidance of Edward Valentine.

The General Sits for a Bust

At the conclusion of his tour of the South, the General returned to Richmond. On May 25, 1870, he endured a session with the artist Edward V. Valentine, who took measurements for a proposed sculptured bust. This was the same artist, now returned from Europe, who had prepared a statuette of the General from photographs made by Julian Vannerson during the war. According to newspaper reports, this project had been in the planning stage as early as December 1865.[3] Valentine recorded 22 different measurements of the five-foot eleven-inches tall Lee, such as thickness of the lip and distance between the eyes, in what must have been a very tedious process.[4] Lee left Richmond the next day, having made arrangements for Valentine to come to Lexington to complete his model. Within a couple of weeks, Valentine was ready to work in a makeshift studio in Lexington. "On one occasion," Valentine stated, "while General Lee never posed himself, I thought it would be to my advantage to secure pictures of him in different positions. He kindly consented to go to a photo-

graph gallery and I had several taken of him." Valentine made the observation that "Every artist of experience in portraiture appreciates the advantage of being able to work from a costume which he knows has been worn by the subject he has to represent."[5]

Valentine and Lee went to Michael Miley's establishment. Although this session is well documented, no photographs of Lee have been definitely attributed to it; there are, however, some likely prospects. One would expect a sculptor to need views of several poses. However, Valentine already had several copies of wartime photographs from which to work, and perhaps needed only two or three additional photographs.

There are two images of Lee standing erect which have long been attributed to Michael Miley circa 1868-69. Both Meredith and a later student of Lee photographs, David J. Eicher, presumed, because of similarities, that they were made at the same session. The movable background and drapery are identical in each. One is a near left profile of the General standing almost painfully erect. He wears a dark suit, the coat having a notched lapel. A watch chain is visible across the left side of the vest. His rather narrow bow tie reveals a small amount of his white shirt collar above his tie, underneath his chin. The bottom edge/corner of the rather narrow white collar is easily seen above his left lapel. His hair and beard are neatly trimmed. The other standing photograph shows the General looking almost straight forward.

Lee seems to be in identical attire for each photograph, except for a heretofore unmentioned detail. He is wearing two different coats! One is a sack coat, the bottom of which ends at his fingertips, while the other is a frock coat, slightly pinched at the waist. It is a longer (three-quarter-length) coat, perhaps more of a military cut, extending well down his thighs. The shorter coat has notched lapels; the longer one, slightly

peaked lapels. These photographs were either taken at different sessions in the same studio or, more likely, Lee changed coats to give the sculptor a little different perspective.

A change of wardrobe in mid-session supports the conclusion that this was no ordinary photographic sitting. Excerpts taken from a letter written by Lee's wife to Edward Valentine underscores the importance of the sculptor having access to clothing actually worn by the subject. On September 29, 1870, she wrote:

A full length photograph of General Lee made by Michael Miley in Lexington, Virginia, in June 1870, for the use of Edward V. Valentine as a pattern for his sculpture, labeled for purposes of this manuscript "Pose 2." Valentine Richmond History Center

I fear you will think me very neglectful of your wishes for indeed as soon as the Genl returned I spoke to him about the coat. He has only one and the buttons have been changed and one inserted between each two of the uniform buttons. There were also three stars on the collar, two small and a large one in the middle. I suppose you have seen many Confederate uniforms and can readily supply all that is necessary. I sent the coat down to Miley's where it has been for some time as the General thought it best to have that rear picture you wanted taken in that coat but he has never found time to go, he has been so continually occupied and now he is so sick, the consequences I think of over exertion that it is useless to keep you waiting any longer, so I will ask Mr. Miley tomorrow to express the coat to you at once. Please take good care of it as I may like to preserve it. I hope soon to hear you have succeeded as well with your full length figure as you have with your bust.[6]

Both of these rigidly posed photographs were evidently made at the same photographic session in Miley's gallery in June 1870, under the direction of Edward Valentine. When viewing the photograph of Lee with his right arm propped on the table, it takes little imagination to see a similar position of his arm as it lies across his torso in Valentine's famous statue of the recumbent

General. There may be other photographs that can be reasonably assigned to this sitting.

A carbon-print version of the image of Lee standing in his sack coat, cropped to remove about one-quarter of the image, still measures six by eight inches, suggesting that the original negative measured at least eight by ten inches. This large format would be expected if these were indeed to be used by Valentine as patterns for his statue. Smaller versions of

A cropped version of Michael Miley's 1870 "Pose 1" standing print originally made as a model for the sculptor Edward Valentine in Lexington, Virginia, and produced later as a carbon print. Donald A. Hopkins

these images should not be considered to be "from life" images of Lee.

Carbon-Print Photographs

Carbon printing was a photographic technique that evolved in the mid-1860s. A sheet of paper was prepared with a layer of light-sensitive gelatin containing a permanent pigment, usually carbon (lamp black). This paper was then exposed through a negative to sunlight. The sensitized gelatin hardened in proportion to the amount of light it received through the negative. The softer gelatin/carbon areas were then washed away, leaving the picture as exposed.

The result was a photograph with a matte finish with great resistance to fading. Carbon-print photographs were often used as "tipped in" photographs in books or for other commercial uses.[7] Carbon prints were usually black and white, but sometimes they were produced in colors by a rather complicated system using different colored material in layers. Michael Miley was a pioneer in this technique.

Notes
Chapter 13: The Final Years

[1] Edward V. Valentine, "Reminiscences of General Lee," in Franklin L. Riley, ed., *General Robert E. Lee after Appomattox* (New York, NY, 1922), 146.

[2] Old typescript note attached to back of original period framed photograph in author's collection.

[3] Gorman, "Civil War Richmond" (Richmond, VA, 2008). http://www.mdgorman.com/Written_Accounts/newspape.htm

[4] "Untitled Tabulation in E. V. Valentine's Hand," Manuscript Collection 57, Valentine Richmond History Center, Richmond, VA.

[5] Riley, *Lee after Appomattox*, 151.

[6] Mary Custis Lee to Edward V. Valentine, September 29, 1870, Manuscript Collection 57, Valentine Richmond History Center.

[7] "Tipped in" refers to the technique of attaching an illustration, usually a print or photograph, by one edge into a publication. It was a common practice during the days when printing processes could only accommodate line drawings.

CHAPTER 14

MYSTERIES OF TIME AND PLACE

*"He was dressed in his plain grey clothes,
with his cavalry boots, and mounted upon his grey charger,
the same noble animal that had borne his master
in many a fearful conflict. . . ."*[1]

Presenting a plausible scenario regarding the origins of the last few photographs presented in this volume requires that facts be melded with general circumstances. Ultimately, what artist made these pictures, and under what circumstances, remains a mystery.

The Elusive Photograph from Baltimore

Beginning in December 1865, General Lee and Reverend S. D. Stuart exchanged extensive correspondence regarding fundraising for Washington College. The letters provide some information regarding photographs. Reverend Stuart wrote to Lee from Baltimore: "And now my Dear Sir I wish in concluding to ask some small favor. . . . That you furnish me a number of your autographs in such form as will so to be cut-off & pasted under a likeness of you. . . . Many of your friends are greatly desirous of having them in this form & I trust you will not esteem too small a troublesome a matter to allow me to furnish them this gratification. . . ."[2]

Stuart wrote again from Baltimore three months later, in mid-March 1866:

I take the opportunity of communicating to you a message of kind remembrances from Mrs. James Robb now of New York, who has a warm Southern heart & like all our Southern women a sincere admiration for you. I had promised her a likeness of you on a carte-visite with your autograph. She said she would prefer receiving it from you. I enclose one which I had gotten up here & which I think rather better than any other that I have seen of you — Should like to have the opinion of your family upon it. If you have one that you think better please let Mrs. Robb have it & oblige me also with a copy. . . .[3]

General Lee responded shortly after, on March 16, 1866: "I enclose to you my photograph for Mrs. James Robb, which I infer from your letter she desired, as I do not know her address. I also send one to you as you requested. The one taken by Mr. P. L. Perkins which you sent for my signature is not considered good."[4]

This correspondence with Stuart brings up a tantalizing question. What image was "taken by Mr. P. L. Perkins," a well-known photographer of Baltimore, and available for purchase before mid-March 1866? Of course, Perkins might have either taken a photograph of Lee himself or made and sold copies of someone else's work. But General Lee's letter clearly states that the photograph was "taken by Mr. P. L. Perkins."

Lee had many friends and relatives in Baltimore, and on any of several visits could have had his photograph taken. Within the first year after the war ended, however, the only opportunity that Lee had to go to Baltimore was when he went to Washington, D.C., for the Senate hearings in February 1866, at which time he had photographs made by Alexander Gardner and Mathew Brady. Douglas Southall Freeman's biography of Lee includes a newspaper account that the General did indeed go to Baltimore on this trip, a possibility that Freeman did not consider seriously. Further investigation reveals, however, that two different newspapers, *Daily Dispatch* on February 14 and *The Daily News* of Lynchburg on February 15, each independently referenced an article which had appeared in the *Baltimore Sun* a few days earlier. The news reports noted that Lee stayed with a relative in Baltimore and attended Sunday services at St. Paul's Church.[5]

Lee evidently left home no later than early Saturday, February 10, yet did not arrive in Washington until the late afternoon of February 16, a span of nearly a week. The trip from Lexington to either Washington or Baltimore ordinarily took less than two days. Where was General Lee during these extra three or four days? One logical answer is Baltimore, less than half a day's rail ride away from Washington, D.C. There was

ample time for Lee to have a photograph made in Baltimore.

General Lee clearly expressed in his correspondence with Alexander Gardner a few weeks later that he preferred unmarked photographs; therefore, the lack of a picture bearing the fancy Perkins imprint is no surprise. Also, Lee flatly stated to Reverend Stuart that the Perkins image "is not considered good," and evidently refused to sign it. What photograph was this?

During the war Lee did not at any time go to Baltimore. Also, it is not likely that Perkins would have made copies of photographs made at the only three postwar sittings Lee had participated in up to this time. Brady had taken his photographs in April 1865 and February 1866, and the Gardner photographs also were made only a month prior to the March 1866 letter to Reverend Stuart. Both Brady and Gardner were careful to

A photograph without a photographer's imprint possibly made by P. L. Perkins of Baltimore in 1866, and later used as a model for a painting of General Lee by John Dabour. North South Trader Magazine

A pastel portrait by John Dabour of Baltimore painted after 1870 which was based on a photograph possibly taken by P. L. Perkins of Baltimore in 1866. Washington and Lee University

in recent years which could possibly have been made there. Though in very poor condition, it is a chest view with the General facing obliquely to his left. A brief article in the *North South Trader* magazine related this particular image to a fine painting of Lee now at Washington and Lee University. The writers of the article speculated that the easily visualized damage to the borders of the photograph was caused by tape used to hold it in place for an artist to use as a model, certainly a reasonable assumption judging by the pattern of the damage.[6] Unfortunately, the original photograph shown in the magazine in 1985, which had no photographer's imprint, is no longer available, its whereabouts unknown.[7] The photograph illustrated in the magazine is almost indistinguish-

copyright their work, and in addition Lee heaped praise on Gardner's photographs and is not recorded as objecting to the results of Brady's work. Lee had given tacit approval of every known wartime photograph by signing and presenting examples of each to his friends and relatives. If a "from life" image of Lee made by Perkins surfaces, it seems likely that it will be an unflattering image, probably unsigned by the General, and likely with no photographer's imprint.

There is indeed one photograph with a very tenuous, indirect connection to Baltimore which seems to meet these criteria. A somewhat mysterious photograph surfaced

A carte de visite with a Michael Miley, Lexington, Virginia, imprint bearing an enhanced copy of the Robert E. Lee photograph, the original of which may have been made by P. L. Perkins of Baltimore in 1866. Washington and Lee University

able from a well-known pastel portrait of Lee. The portrait was commissioned by General Lee's wartime aide, Walter H. Taylor, whose family later presented it to Washington and Lee University. There is no documentation whatsoever that Lee ever sat for this painting, and in fact most authorities have now concluded that the artist based his painting on a photograph. The artist, John Dabour from Smyrna, Turkey, opened his gallery in Baltimore in about 1870. He may have obtained the photograph locally, perhaps from Palmer Lenfield Perkins. Roy Meredith notes that, although there is no record of Lee ever sitting for this painting, he could have done so during his visit to Baltimore in the spring of 1869.[8] At the time Meredith expressed this opinion (1947), the painting had not yet been traced to a specific photograph of Lee.

This painting most certainly was modeled after a photograph. A carte de visite copy of a heavily enhanced vignetted view (without a Lee signature) of the same photograph illustrated in the magazine article is found in the archives at Washington and Lee. It has a presentation date of March 28, 1868, in period manuscript on the verso, establishing that it was made before the General visited Baltimore in 1869. This carte de visite with a Michael Miley imprint had previously been attributed to Michael Miley "sometime late in the 1860s." However, as noted earlier, it was quite common for Miley to place his imprint on copies of other photographers' work, especially photographs of Robert E. Lee. He even photographed oil and pastel portraits of General Lee as he experimented with color photography.

Until this photograph is more conclusively attributed, this author considers it to have been made in February 1866 by P. L. Perkins of Baltimore, and later used as a model by John Dabour for his pastel portrait.

Palmer Lenfield Perkins

Palmer Lenfield Perkins was born in New Jersey. He studied photography in Philadelphia, and by 1846 he had established his own daguerreotype studio in Baltimore. He was located in the Franklin Building on the corner of North Street and Baltimore Street in 1850, with his business named "Perkins & Brother Galleries" in 1852.[9] He maintained his photographic business at this location for several years, but by 1884 was listed as being in the insurance business.

Perkins' wartime cartes de visite were primarily of Union soldiers and generally carried a rather elaborate imprint. He was succeeded in business by his son, Harry L. Perkins.

The Lynchburg Photograph

In between two trips to Richmond, on May 20, 1868, Lee traveled to Lynchburg to attend a meeting of the Council of the Protestant Episcopal Church of Virginia. Although he remained there for only two or three days, he did have enough time to have a photograph taken. A very poor copy of a rather unique portrait of Lee is found in the Museum of the Confederacy, without provenance, bearing a backmark of (illegible) and Van Ness of Lynchburg. It was copied long ago, while under glass—i.e., without being removed from some type of composition frame. The location of the original is unknown. According to a very old note accompanying the picture, Mrs. Lee penned a manuscript presentation on the back of the photograph to "John E. C. T. Burwell from his cousin."

The straightforward pose, with bow tie askew, does not match up, at least in fine details of wardrobe—such as the size of Lee's bow tie, the relationship between the step in his coat lapel and the point of his left shoulder, and the configuration of his waistcoat—

with any other known portrait of Lee thus far examined. Lee's face also seems thinner and somewhat more haggard than in earlier photographs. This indistinct photocopy is included here for the sake of completeness. For lack of better evidence, attribution is to Tanner and Van Ness, possibly made during the May 1868 visit to Lynchburg. This photograph certainly deserves further study and research.

Tanner and Van Ness

N. S. Tanner was recorded as a daguerreian in Hillsborough, NC, as early as 1852 or 1853.[10] He later operated an ambrotype gallery in Lynchburg, Virginia. He continued his work in Lynchburg during the early days of wet-plate photography, and in mid-1861 broadened his business by offering photographic supplies, which were already becoming scarce in the newly formed Confederacy. His studio in Lynchburg remained active for several years after the war. Not long after the conflict ended he collaborated with Rockwell of Petersburg on a copy of the Military Medallion.

James H. Van Ness, a veteran of the Confederate Army, formed a partnership with Tanner shortly after the end of hostilities.

A poor reproduction of a rare photograph of Robert E. Lee with a Tanner and Van Ness, Lynchburg, Virginia, backmark possibly made circa 1868. Museum of the Confederacy

Their backmark placed their studio at 124 Main Street, Lynchburg. This business relationship allowed for Van Ness to obtain the necessary on-the-job training as a photographer under Tanner. In addition to their business in portraiture, they marketed many copy portraits of Confederate officers and assorted stereo views.

Although maintaining a base in Lynchburg, in about 1867 Van Ness began to travel from community to community in Virginia and the Carolinas, much like the itinerant Adam Plecker. From 1870 to 1875, he circulated between Charlotte, North Carolina, and Lynchburg, finally settling in Charlotte.

Fincastle Wartime Girls

An uncommon photograph which cannot be precisely dated has in the past been attributed to Michael Miley. Evidently this was based on the fact that a copy of another photograph in the Virginia Historical Society, obviously made at the same sitting, bears a note on its verso that it is from "the Miley Collection." It should be remembered, however, that Miley typically placed his imprint or blind stamp on all of his work, both large- and small-format, whether it was his original work or a copy of some other artist's work.

A photograph of General Lee without a photographer's imprint, labeled "Pose 1" for purposes of this manuscript, used for the center medallion of a composite called "Fincastle Wartime Girls." Virginia Polytechnic Institute and State University

The enhanced image in question shows Lee facing slightly to the left wearing a jacket with somewhat rounded lapels and a bulky, slightly droopy bow tie. There is no photographer's imprint.

An equally rare photograph of General Lee which was obviously taken at the same time has thus far not been credited to a specific photographic artist. The photographs are so similar as to almost appear to be mirror images. However, careful examination of details such as the left end of the bow tie's relationship to his lapel and the slight difference in the angle of Lee's head are enough evidence to support a conclusion

that this is indeed a second pose from the same sitting. This vignetted photograph is heavily enhanced.

"Pose 1" has been found as a center medallion of a composite photograph entitled "Fincastle Wartime Girls" in which Lee's portrait is surrounded by 12 portraits of young ladies, presumably from Fincastle, Virginia.[11] Fincastle was a small independent community located in Botetourt County, which adjoins Rockbridge County not far from Lexington. An old photographic copy of this collage found in the Virginia Historical Society's Miley Collection is stamped on the verso "Library, University of Richmond, Virginia." An exhaustive search in and around Fincastle has produced no original print or negative of these photographs. This composite, by its

A greatly enhanced large format photograph of General Lee, circa 1869, without a photographer's imprint, is labeled "Pose 2" for purposes of this manuscript. Dementi Studio

bon around the border is made of some type of cloth ribbon (called rickrack by my grandmother), joined together by stitches. Lee's photograph, trimmed to an oval, was placed in the center. The appearance of stars was cleverly created by cutting individual bits of white paper into proper shapes and then gluing them in position on the background around each girl's photograph to simulate a six-pointed star surrounding each one's face. Once constructed, it was then photographed. Adam Plecker, with whom Michael Miley had worked briefly in 1866, was still

A cropped and enlarged view of the composite "Fincastle Wartime Girls" showing construction details. Virginia Historical Society

An undated example of the composite photograph by an unknown photographer called "Fincastle Wartime Girls" with General Lee's photograph as the center medallion. Virginia Historical Society

design, seems to have been made up as a "craft" project, perhaps by some of the young ladies pictured, rather than the product of a professional photographic artist.

Close examination reveals small irregularities indicating that the spiculated black, oval framing the collage was neatly done by hand. The overlay of light-colored undulating rib-

moving about as an itinerant photographer until several years after the death of Robert E. Lee. Then he parked his traveling gallery and established a permanent studio in Lynchburg. He also at some

1866, for the *Confederate Veteran* magazine in 1922, Plecker stated, "My recollection of the short acquaintance with General [Lee] at the Baths, with his daughters in the ballroom, and of Mrs. Lee at her home in Lexington, Virginia, are very pleasant memories."[12] Although this magazine article written by Plecker focused on one specific photographic session with General Lee, it does not rule out a later encounter.

Non-vignetted carte de visite portrait, "Pose 2," bearing an Adam Plecker imprint.
Douglas York

point set up studios in Salem and Fincastle, Virginia. If Plecker happened to be the artist who made these photographs while working from his traveling van, he could have photographed General Lee at any location within a three- or four-county area surrounding Lexington. When commenting specifically on events surrounding and immediately following his photographic session with General Lee and his horse at Rockbridge Baths in

Verso of carte de visite portrait, "Pose 2," showing Adam Plecker's imprint. Douglas York

In fact, carte de visite versions of "Pose 2" have been found imprinted with Adam Plecker's Traveling Gallery, and no other imprints or backmarks have as yet been found on either of these two photographic poses. This Plecker-imprinted photograph is not vignetted but shows drapery in the background, strongly suggesting that it is a copy of the original "from life" pose.

Consider the limited regional interest this composite of pictures of local ladies would be expected to generate; then contrast it with the interest throughout the entire old Confederacy, and even the North, for another composite with Lee as the center medallion—the 1866 Military Medallion. The photograph showing "girls" from the rural Fincastle, Virginia, area arranged around Lee's portrait certainly must have been made for local consumption, perhaps to be sold by a local women's organization, Confederate veterans group, or church group. It seems very likely that the Fincastle Wartime Girls collage was handcrafted from individual photographs before being taken to a photographer to be photographed. Of course, each of the ladies would have had access to her own wartime photographs, but the origin of the photographs of Lee remains somewhat uncertain.

After the war, Lee made visits of several days each to Washington, Baltimore, Richmond, Petersburg, Norfolk, Rockbridge Baths, White Sulphur Springs, and Savannah, all being locations where he is known or thought to have had photographs made. A detailed study of Robert E. Lee biographies reveals only an additional handful of postwar visits of at least two or three days' duration to communities with established photographic studios. These two photographs could have been made during one of these brief sojourns to any of these communities, which included Alexandria, Lynchburg, and Staunton. However, more times than not the brevity or the timing of the visit did not allow for a sitting. Photographers of the day required a considerable period of natural daylight to obtain suitable photographs.

In February 1866, following his first trip to Washington after the war, the General returned via Alexandria, where he spent five or six days. This was certainly enough time to have his picture made. However, he had just completed sittings for Alexander Gardner and Mathew Brady in Washington, and a comparison of Lee's facial features, hair, and beard in these pictures alongside their work seems to negate the possibility of both sets being taken within a few days of each other.

A previous discussion addressed the possibility that Tanner and Van Ness made a photograph of the General during his journey to Lynchburg in May 1868. However, these two photographs bear no resemblance to the photograph with the Tanner and Van Ness backmark, either in facial features or wardrobe, and certainly were not made at the same sitting.

Local newspapers such as the *Valley Virginian* and the *Staunton Spectator* reported in late October and early November 1868 that General Lee, along with many other distinguished persons such as Commodore Maury, was in attendance at the Augusta County Fair. This was a several-day event held at Staunton, and Lee might well have visited a local photographer in Staunton during this visit. His final visit to Staunton was nearly a year later at the end of August, extending into September, 1870, on railroad business. He again had time between business meetings to have a photograph made. Any one of his extended summer visits to Rockbridge Baths or White Sulphur Springs, where photographers commonly plied their craft, could have resulted in these photographs. Because Adam Plecker's Traveling Gallery imprint is the only one so far found on either version of these two poses, they must tentatively be assigned to him as the original artist.

Perhaps these two photographs are so scarce because they were specifically commissioned for inclusion in these collages rather than for widespread distribution. General

Lee, with his well-known fondness for children and young ladies, could have been easily enticed to sit for a photographer in order to assist the young women with their project.

In summary, it seems likely that, after fabrication around a central portrait of General Lee, most likely made by Adam Plecker, this postwar composite was photographed in an unknown studio near Fincastle, Virginia, for limited distribution.

The "Norfolk" Photograph

During his southern tour in the spring of 1870, Lee spent a short time in Savannah before leaving the Georgia city in mid-April for a three-day excursion farther south. Lee's party returned to Savannah for another nine days before traveling back to Virginia. Their tiresome return journey took them through Norfolk, where they spent several days during the end of April and the first part of May.[13] A soiled and faded letter written by Robert E. Lee's wife on September 29, 1870, shortly before his death, clearly indicates that he had a photograph made in Norfolk, possibly during this brief visit. The letter, found in the archives of the Valentine Richmond History Center, was written to the sculptor Edward V. Valentine. Mrs. Lee refers to a photograph made in Norfolk in the following excerpts: "The photograph from Norfolk I think the best for the figure and the most military of any that have been

taken. The Genl is more bent now but I would preserve him perfectly erect as he was during and before the War. I should like to have a few cartes de visites from that photograph. I have so many applications and – wanting for them – the original negative is lost."[14]

A print made from an original negative, previously attributed to Michael Miley of Lexington, Virginia, showing General Lee's military-like erectness, which may actually be one of the "Norfolk Photographs" labeled "Pose 1" for purposes of this manuscript.
Dementi Studio

During his early service as an engineer in the U.S. Army, Lee did spend some time in and around Norfolk. However, this was in the early 1830s, well before the advent of wet-plate photography. Mrs. Lee's reference to a "negative" clearly dates this photograph to the mid-1850s or later. There is no record

that Lee visited Norfolk during the war except for a very brief two-day period in June 1861 when he was inspecting the defenses on the peninsula. The visit in May 1870 was apparently his only opportunity to sit for a photographer in Norfolk after the war ended. No other written account of Lee sitting for a portrait in Norfolk has thus far surfaced, and no photograph or group of photographs can be definitively assigned to a Norfolk artist.

A print made from a damaged negative, or either a copy print of a damaged photographic print, previously attributed to Michael Miley of Lexington, Virginia, showing General Lee's military-like erectness, which may actually be one of the "Norfolk Photographs" labeled "Pose 1" for purposes of this manuscript. Valentine Richmond History Center

A search through all known photographs of Robert E. Lee for this Norfolk Photograph leads to only a small number of images which have no firm attribution as to artist and date. All of his known wartime photographs in uniform may be ruled out, since they have all been definitively classified as to artist and/or the time and place they were made, and none were made in Norfolk. The search quickly narrows to finding a heretofore unattributed postwar portrait that illustrates his erect military bearing. If indeed the negative of the photograph Mrs. Lee describes was broken by September 1870, it likely will not be an image widely familiar to historians and collectors. Furthermore, in Mrs. Lee's letter to Edward Valentine she refers to this photograph without explanation, which indicates that the sculptor was already familiar with this Norfolk Photograph. The meager clues contained in Mrs. Lee's letter seem to be the only evidence of a Robert E. Lee photograph made in Norfolk.

Prints made from glass-plate negatives found both in the Dementi Studio collection in Richmond and the Valentine Richmond History Center's Cook Collection in Richmond are worthy of consideration. One of these otherwise identical prints suggests that

the negative from which it was made was damaged, or alternately the print was damaged during development. A copy of this same photograph in carte de visite format found in the Valentine Richmond History Center bears no photographer's imprint, but has a note on the back in Edward Valentine's hand dating the picture to the "last two or three years of Lee's life." This notation confirms that Valentine was certainly familiar with this particular portrait of the General. The erect, stiff pose of this waist-

An additional pose from the "Norfolk" sitting bearing a D. H. Anderson, Richmond, Virginia, imprint, labeled "Pose 3" for purposes of this manuscript. Douglas York

An additional pose from the "Norfolk" sitting bearing a D. H. Anderson, Richmond, Virginia, imprint, labeled "Pose 2" for purposes of this manuscript. Gilder Lehrman Institute of American History

up view could easily be construed to represent the pose described by Mrs. Lee. Details of Lee's wardrobe confirm that this photograph was made during the same sitting as those pictures, discussed earlier, which were used as models for the print found in *The Davis Memorial Volume* published in 1890.

There seems to be enough collective, albeit mostly circumstantial, evidence to conclude that these three portraits include the Norfolk Photograph, as described by Mrs. Lee. Who, then, was the photographer?

This group of three portraits, like so many others, has often been attributed to Michael Miley, circa 1868, apparently without a firm basis in fact. Miley has been given credit for many photographs known to have been made by other artists simply because he usually placed his imprint on his photographs whether they were his original work or a copy of some other artist's work. It is significant that none of the three photographs assigned to this sitting have been found with a Michael Miley imprint.

Even though the Cook Collection contains prints made from glass-plate negatives of one of these images, George Cook never took a "from life" photograph of Lee. He did amass a huge collection of glass-plate negatives when he moved to Richmond and bought out D. H. Anderson and later purchased the Lee Gallery inventory, which included not only negatives made by the Davies family but also those they had purchased earlier from Julian Vannerson.

Only the imprints of D. H. Anderson of Richmond and W. W. Davies of the Lee Gallery in Richmond have been noted on some of these rare cartes de visite. Anderson, who began work in Richmond in 1866, could have made these portraits as originals anytime during the last four years of Lee's life. If Davies made the original photographs, it would have been during the final months of Lee's life, because the Lee Gallery did not come into existence until sometime in 1869. A third possible photographer to consider is Julian Vannerson, who had very close ties to both Davies and Anderson. Vannerson sold his business, including negatives, prints, and equipment, to Davies in 1869 and left Richmond, evidently for Norfolk. He is known to have been working with Anderson in Norfolk as late as 1875. Furthermore, Julian Vannerson was well acquainted with General Lee, having made the famous Blockade Portraits for Edward Valentine in 1863. A plausible case can be made that this photograph of General Lee, showing a very erect pose with shoulders "squared away," was made in Norfolk in May 1870, perhaps by Julian Vannerson while he was working alone or working with D. H. Anderson.

The photographs from this sitting for an unknown artist have been dubbed the Norfolk Photograph herein based upon very circumstantial evidence. Perhaps further research will definitively establish the date they were taken and the location of the artist's gallery.

Notes
Chapter 14: Mysteries of Time and Place

[1] A local reporter comments on the appearance of Robert E. Lee in late 1868. – "Augusta County Fair," *Staunton (VA) Spectator*, November 10, 1868. http://www2.vcdh.virginia.edu/saxon/servlet/

[2] S. D. Stuart to Robert E. Lee, December 27, 1865, Leyburn Library, Washington and Lee University.

[3] S. D. Stuart to Robert E. Lee, March 14, 1866, Leyburn Library, Washington and Lee University.

[4] Robert E. Lee to Rev. S. D. Stuart, March 16, 1866, Leyburn Library, Washington and Lee University.

[5] Freeman, Robert E. Lee, vol. 4, 256. "Gen. Lee in Baltimore," *The Daily News* (Lynchburg, VA), February 15, 1866.

[6] Mike O'Donnell and Steve Sylvia, "Unknown Lee Photo Found!" *North South Trader* (September-October 1985), 29.

[7] Steve Sylvia, ed., *North South Trader*, telephone interview in 2010.

[8] Meredith, *The Face of Robert E. Lee*, 131.

[9] Craig, "P. L. Perkins," in *Craig's Daguerreian Registry*.

[10] Craig, "N. S. Tanner," in *Craig's Daguerreian Registry*.

[11] "Robert E. Lee with Fincastle Wartime Girls," Museum No. 2001.2.31, Virginia Historical Society.

[12] Plecker, "General Lee on Traveler," 117.

[13] Fishwick, *Lee After the War*, 1963.

[14] Mary Custis Lee to Edward V. Valentine, September 29, 1870, Manuscript Collection 57, Valentine Richmond History Center.

CHAPTER 15

THE LEGEND LIVES ON

"That picture of peace represents exquisitely the genius of the artist and the greatness of the soldier."[1]

Events surrounding the death of Robert E. Lee on October 12, 1870, were well documented photographically, primarily by Michael Miley. Photographs of all things related to this Southern icon remained in demand for decades. Copies of his existing photographs were sold by the thousands, and even today these period images of the old warrior and his surroundings demand high prices.

Recumbent on the Field of Battle

Michael Miley, and later his son Henry, along with Edward V. Valentine continued to produce classic Robert E. Lee-related artwork for several years after Lee's death. Miley's photographs of Valentine's statue of a recumbent Lee in the chapel at Washington and Lee University proved to be a commercial success.[2] Originally made as albumen silver prints, they were later presented in various formats and sizes using more modern techniques.

The bereaved South proved to be a ready market for the many photographic memorials to their beloved General. Carte de visite-size cards, in countless variations, bearing small photographs, engravings, or prints of Lee surrounded by Confederate flags, religious symbols, and Victorian artwork, sold by the thousands.

A few entrepreneurs published larger format cards or prints with an open medallion in the center where any one of the photographs of Lee could be trimmed to a circle or oval and pasted.

An unmarked photograph showing Robert E. Lee lying in state under the watchful eyes of two of his students at Washington College, Lexington, Virginia, October 1870. Washington and Lee University

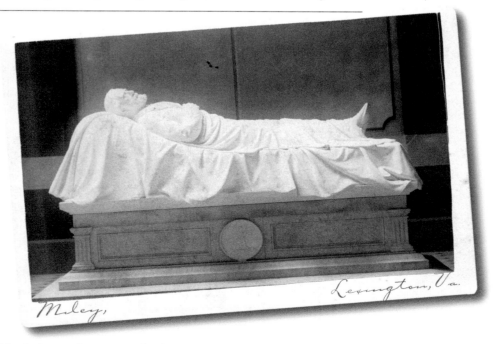

Valentine's recumbent statue of Robert E. Lee as shown in an albumen/silver print made by Michael Miley of Lexington, Virginia, in 1876. Donald A. Hopkins

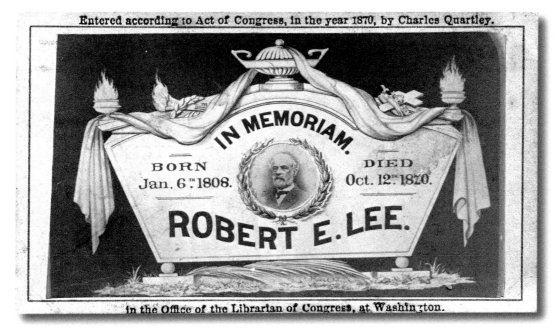

Entered according to Act of Congress, in the year 1870, by Charles Quartley.

IN MEMORIAM.

BORN
Jan. 6ᵗʰ 1808.

DIED
Oct. 12ᵗʰ 1870.

ROBERT E. LEE.

In the Office of the Librarian of Congress, at Washington.

A large format memorial card published by Leach and Edkins, Photographers of Baltimore, Maryland, upon which a real photograph of Robert E. Lee could be fitted into the center medallion. Museum of the Confederacy

Looking Forward

As this narrative concludes, this author hopes that those of an inquisitive nature vis-à-vis historical subjects will continue to re-explore the nooks and crannies of bygone days. The goal should not be to refute the work of past scholars; instead, the aspiration should be to bring forward new facts and make information more widely available than in the past, in order to interweave new information with the old in the interest of historical accuracy. Such an approach is certain to lead in the future to clarification and correction of information presented in this volume.

Notes

Chapter 15: The Legend Lives On

[1] B. A. C. Emerson, comp., *Historic Southern Monuments; Representative Memorials of the Heroic Southern Dead of the Confederacy* (New York and Washington, 1911), 410.

[2] Editor's note, "The Last Roll," *Confederate Veteran Magazine*, Vol. 7, No. 517.

EVOLUTION OF THE DAGUERREOTYPE PORTRAIT

Daguerreotype plates were produced by heating and rolling thin silver foil onto a sheet of copper, a process which resulted in what is today called Sheffield plate. The photograph which is produced directly on the silvered surface is very fragile and can be easily rubbed off—even by one's fingers. Depending on the viewing angle the image appears to change from a positive to a negative. The most important part of the daguerreotype camera being the lens, there was intense competition in the matter of lens design. The earliest practical lens for these cameras was a simple achromatic one designed by Charles-Louis Chevalier of Paris. In 1839, Mr. Chevalier began selling the Giroux daguerreotype camera fitted with a lens he originally designed for microscopes. This type of lens, coupled with a photographic plate made light sensitive with silver iodide proved to be unsatisfactory for portraiture because the required exposure time was too lengthy. In 1840, Joseph Petzval marketed a larger diameter double lens, which, when combined with a plate made light sensitive with both silver bromide and silver iodide, made shorter exposure times possible. This ushered in the era of daguerreotype portraiture. Even with a somewhat shortened exposure time, the sitter was usually required to lean on their elbows on a support, or be submitted to an unobtrusive clamp-like head support so as to remain motionless.

Thermoplastic is one of the earliest forms of plastic made by combining shellac, sawdust, and other chemicals and dyes. The material could be heated then pressed into a mold and allowed to harden into a finished product. The union of these ingredients led the inventor Samuel Peck in 1854 to name the protective daguerreotype cases made from the material "union cases." They usually were black or brown in color. Before the thermoplastic union case was invented, daguerreotype or ambrotype cases were usually made from wood and covered with very thin leather. Sometimes they were made from other materials and covered with mother-of-pearl and silver wire inlay.

Photographic plate size in the nineteenth century was uniform for not only daguerreotypes but for ambrotypes, tintypes, and other photographic formats developed later. The "whole plate" size is about 6½ inches x 8½ inches. The size of smaller photographs was defined by how many plates of the smaller size could be cut from a whole plate, expressed for example as a sixth plate, or the much smaller sixteenth plate. Usually the brass mat placed in front of American photographs measured the same size as the photograph underneath and can be used to identify the plate size of the image without removing the fragile picture from its protective case. Sometimes a photograph was trimmed by the photographer into an oval, circle, or some other shape in order to fit into an oddly shaped case. In such situations the original plate size is considered to be the smallest standard plate size from which the picture could have been cut. On occasion a small photograph was placed in an oversized mat for a more pleasing presentation. Because European photographs of the era were mounted differently it is more difficult to determine the size of these images while in their original mounts or frames.

APPENDIX B

A FAMILY RESEMBLANCE

Sidney Smith Lee was Robert E. Lee's brother, five years older than Robert. Sidney, sometimes spelled "Sydney," had a distinguished career in the U.S. Navy before and during the Mexican War and later with Perry's expedition to the orient. He also served as Superintendent of the U.S. Naval Academy at the same time his brother Robert was Superintendent of the U.S. Military Academy at West Point. Sidney, like his younger brother, was considered very handsome, with a strong family resemblance to Robert. At least one distinguished historian, Dr. John O'Brien, Professor Emeritus, University of Connecticut, Storrs, feels rather strongly that the daguerreotype purported to be Robert E. Lee and his son is actually a photograph of Sidney Smith Lee and his son Fitzhugh Lee. He bases his assertion on the lack of firm documentation from anyone in the Lee family that it is Robert and his son, and upon his analysis of the facial features as shown by the photograph. The author has been unable to confirm Dr. O'Brien's opinion.

APPENDIX C

THE BAZAAR AT LIVERPOOL

Liverpool, England, was generally pro-Confederacy. This could be expected as at least 60% of the Southern states' cotton passed through the port of Liverpool before the outbreak of the Civil War. When the Northern naval blockade became effective it had a huge impact upon trade in Liverpool. Liverpool also made a large amount of money from the slave trade. The region's citizens supported the Southerners' efforts in many ways, including holding benefit fairs and bazaars to aid Southern prisoners. The London Times reported on such an event on October 7, 1864. Edward V. Valentine's statuette of Lee based on the Vannerson photographs was not completed in time to be auctioned or raffled off at this bazaar as planned.

BAZAAR in aid of the SOUTHERN PRISONERS' RELIEF FUND
Lady Patronesses H. I. H. the Princess Murat
The Marchioness of Lothian
The Marchioness of Bath
The Marchioness of Allesbury
La Marquise de Montmort
The Countess of Chesterfield
The Countess of Tankerville
Lady Mildred Beresford Hope
Lady Rosa Greville
The Countess Bentivoglio
Lady Georgina Fane
Lady Eustace Cecil
Lady Warncliffe
La Vicomtesse de Dampierre
La Baronne de Langueil
Lady de Hoghton
Lady Anson
Lady Eardly

Mrs. Horsefall, Liverpool
Mrs. Laird, Birkenhead
Mrs. Akroyd, Halifax
Mrs. Collie, London
Mrs. Hannan, Glasgow

It is intended to hold a BAZAAR in St. Georges Hall, commencing on Tuesday, October 18, in aid of the Southern Prisoners' Relief Fund.

Many ladies, in addition to those named, have promised their active aid. The suffering of the Southern prisoners of war in sickness, wounds, and deprivation of every comfort of life; the multitudes of widows to whom nothing remains, and of orphans unable to help themselves, form an amount of woe which some who are blessed here with an abundance and peace have felt a desire to alleviate. Efforts have already been made, and not without success, through reliable friends in the Northern States, but unhappily the field is wide that aid is now required to replace the means already provided and exhausted. It is hoped that assistance will not be refused in this work, which is wholly one of humanity — of sympathy for the great sorrows and suffering that now afflict a people of our own race.

The stalls of the Southern States will be held by the following ladies:
Virginia:
La Vicomtesse de Dampierre. Mrs. Patterson. Mrs. M. G. Klingender.
N. Carolina:
Mrs. Spence. Mrs. Wothington.
S. Carolina:
The Lady Warncliffe. Mrs. Prioleau.

Georgia:
Mrs. Bulloch. Mrs Patrick.
Alabama:
Mrs. Malcomson. Mrs. Pratt.
Mississippi:
The Countess of Chesterfield.
The Right Hon. Mrs. Sliddell.
Louisiana:
Mrs. Byrne. Mrs. T. Byrne. Mrs. F.Rodewald.
Texas:
Mrs. A. Forwood.
Mrs. W. Forwood. Mrs. W. Heyn.
Arkansas:
Mrs. Sillem. Mrs. J. Wilklink.
Tennessee:
The Lady M. Beresford Hope. Mrs. F. Hull.

Kentucky:
Lady de Hoghton. Mrs. G. W. Oliver.
Treasurer:
CHARLES K. PRIOLEAU.
Hon. Sec.:
JAMES SPENCE Liverpool

A later report by the same newspaper suggests that the good ladies of Liverpool may have substituted a donkey for the statuette!

"Confederate Bazaar - In October 1864 Liverpool staged a bazaar at St. George's hall called the 'Southern Prisoners' Relief Fund'. It lasted for 5 days and raised over £20,000. The stalls included a raffle for a donkey!"[1]

Notes

Appendix C: The Bazaar at Liverpool

[1] "Confederates and their Liverpool Connections," When Liverpool went Dixie. http://www.bbc.co.uk/liverpool/localhistory/journey/american_connection/alabama/bulloch_liverpool.shtml

APPENDIX D

LEE IN PROFILE

Adam Plecker wrote for Confederate Veteran Magazine that the profile view of Robert E. Lee which he noted in Mrs. Lee's fireplace screen was made "by a Washington City photographer" (implying that the sitting occurred in Washington, D.C.).[1] Of course Alexander Gardner's 1866 photographs were made in Washington. Furthermore, in a letter General Lee himself wrote: "The best large one [photograph] I have seen of myself is by Gardner of Washington City; a profile likeness."[2]

After this manuscript had been submitted for publication, Dr. John O'Brien, Emeritus, University of Connecticut, Storrs, called attention to his excellent article published in Military Images in 1986 in which he clearly proves that in addition to the Gardner photographs, Lee had another set of photographs made in Washington during his visit in early 1866. This other photographic session was at Mathew Brady's gallery.[3] Brady made a total of five photographs, which most historians have thought all along were made in early 1869 on Lee's final postwar visit to Washington.

Of Brady's earlier post-war photographs of Lee in his uniform, only one is a profile view, and there is no indication that its negative was broken. In fact, a glass plate negative of this photograph can be found in the Library of Congress. Of course it was taken in Richmond, not Washington. Also, period copies of this particular photograph are by no means "rare." Copies frequently turn up in dealer inventories, at auctions, and in collections. Even with the later, 1866, Brady photographs in the mix, it remains reasonable to conclude that the profile portrait that served as Mrs. Lee's fire screen was the very rare Gardner profile view made in Washington, D.C. in early 1866.

Notes
Appendix D: Lee in Profile

[1] Adam Plecker, "General Lee on Traveler," *Confederate Veteran Magazine* (1970) vol. 30, no. 3, 117.

[2] Robert E. Lee to Reverend William C. Greene, April 15, 1866, Leyburn Library, Washington and Lee University.

[3] John O'Brien, "Brady and Lee, 1866: A History of a Photographic Session," *Military Images*, (March-April 1986), 6-8.

APPENDIX E

PRINTS FROM PHOTOGRAPHS

After reports of Robert E. Lee's exploits during the Mexican War in 1846 began to appear in newspapers, his name became more and more familiar to the reading public. His renown increased even more in 1859 when he led U.S. Marines who captured John Brown during his attempted slave insurrection at Harpers Ferry, Virginia. Editors and publishers noting Lee's rising prominence in military matters, began to seek representative images of him for their readers, and over the next few years woodcuts and steel engravings began to appear in print in both the North and the South.

During the early 1800s, printmakers and engravers primarily based their work on paintings, drawings, or other artistic renderings, but after 1850, they increasingly based their work on photographs of their subject. Engravings of Lee that appeared in print in the U.S. during this time were no different.

Eng'd by A. H. Ritchie.

Steel engraving by A. H. Ritchie based on "West Point" photograph. Published as a photograph in 1861. Donald A. Hopkins

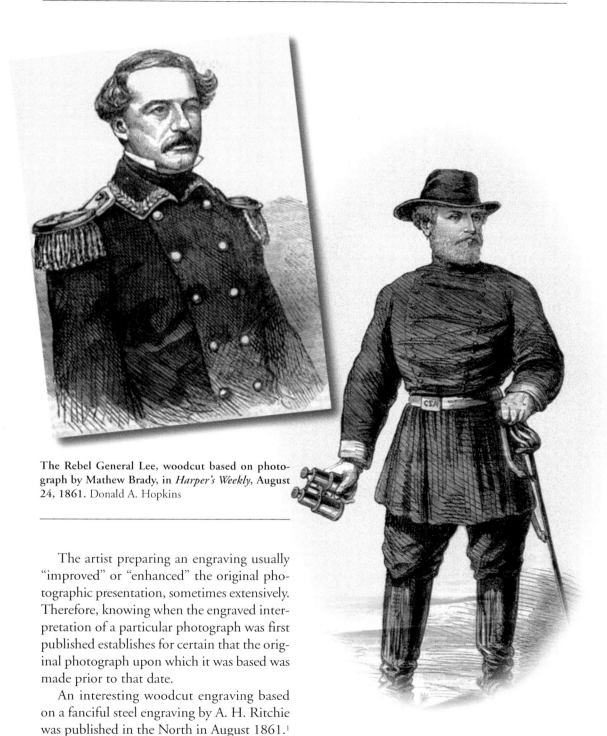

The Rebel General Lee, woodcut based on photo-graph by Mathew Brady, in *Harper's Weekly*, August 24, 1861. Donald A. Hopkins

The artist preparing an engraving usually "improved" or "enhanced" the original pho-tographic presentation, sometimes extensively. Therefore, knowing when the engraved inter-pretation of a particular photograph was first published establishes for certain that the orig-inal photograph upon which it was based was made prior to that date.

An interesting woodcut engraving based on a fanciful steel engraving by A. H. Ritchie was published in the North in August 1861.[1] According to the publisher this woodcut en-graving was derived from a photograph by Mathew Brady.

Engraving based on sketch by Frank Vizetelly for the *Illustrated London News*, February 14, 1863. Virginia Historical Society

During the Civil War there was at least one woodcut engraving of General Lee based on a drawing made in the field, rather than a photograph. In late 1862 or early 1863, Frank Vizetelly of the Illustrated London News sketched General Lee at his headquarters near Fredericksburg.[2]

It is quite possible (the author considers it likely) that Vizetelly's drawing was made a few weeks before General Lee donned his dress uniform for the so-called "Booted and Spurred" photograph made by Daniel T. Cowell. General Lee was not known to have worn such formal military attire except on special occasions. A woodcut engraving derived from Minnis and Cowell's "Booted and Spurred" photograph appeared on the front of Harper's Weekly in July 1864. Oddly enough Lee's middle name "Edward" was misspelled as "Edmund" in the caption of this illustration.[3]

Examination of a well-known print of General Lee as a civilian shows him seated in a comfortable looking chair. It is obviously derived from the famous "Clock Portrait" made in early 1866 by Mathew Brady of Washington, D.C. For years, this sitting for Brady in Washington was deemed to have occurred in 1869. However, this print, published in *Frank Leslie's Illustrated Newspaper*, firmly estab-

lishes that the photograph was made before March 24, 1866.

These printed engravings are quite interesting when compared alongside their corresponding photographs. Those printed in dated periodical publications can help determine the time period when the original photograph was taken.

The Rebel General Robert Edmund Lee, *Harper's Weekly,* July 2, 1864. Donald A. Hopkins

**Engraving based on Mathew Brady's "Clock Portrait"
of 1866 in** *Frank Leslie's Illustrated Newspaper,* **March
24, 1866.** Donald A. Hopkins

Notes

Appendix E: Prints from Photographs

[1] "The Rebel General Lee" [Photographed by Brady],
Harper's Weekly, August 24, 1861, 541.

[2] "The Civil War in America: General Lee Commander
of the Confederate Army in Northern Virginia-From
Sketch by our Special Artist," *Illustrated London News,*
February 14, 1863, 185.

[3] "The Rebel General Robert Edmund Lee," *Harper's
Weekly,* A Journal of Civilization, July 2, 1864, 1.

AN INTERVIEW WITH AUTHOR DONALD A. HOPKINS

Q: *Why did you decide to write a photography book about Robert E. Lee?*

A: I have had a lifelong interest in Southern history, the American Civil War, and historical research in general. Naturally, I began to accumulate related artifacts, documents, and photographs of the period for my own collection. As years went by I began to buy and sell such items at collector's shows and antique shops. Two facts began to stand out:

1. The "go to" source, or bible if you will, relating to photographs of Robert E. Lee is a well-known book first published in 1947. If I wanted to know who made a photograph of Lee or when it was made, I was directed to check it out in Roy Meredith's, *The Face of Robert E. Lee in Life and Legend.*

2. When I began seriously studying Lee photographs, I noted that many inaccuracies and omissions of this book have simply been carried forward by later authors without the benefit of more research. Therefore, many of the period photographs found on the tables at shows and in the showcases of well-known dealers were improperly described with respect to date and photographer. It appeared to me that an updated reference on photographs of Robert E. Lee would be timely, as well as an interesting research project.

Q: What makes Robert E. Lee in War and Peace unique from other books on the same topic?

A: It is a more complete atlas of Robert E. Lee photographs than any other. All currently known life images of the General are presented, many more than in any other volume. Also, for the first time, a book on Lee photographs discusses in some detail the photographic techniques used. Interestingly, Lee's adult life paralleled the development of photography in America; therefore you see photographs of him using the different techniques available at the time. Much more information on his photographers, both northern and southern, is presented than in other books on this topic as well.

Q: *What are some features of your book that you think readers will really enjoy?*

A: In general, I believe they will like my chronological arrangement of the photographs, from the earliest known to the last photograph taken in his life, each discussed in detail as to who took it and when, as well as a discussion which outlines how I reached my conclusions. Furthermore, it is readily apparent that Savas Beatie LLC spared no expense in producing beautiful images for the book.

Q: *Is there anything controversial in your book?*

A: Yes. There are always naysayers and doubters when their ingrained beliefs are challenged, especially if their treasured photograph is not what they thought as reflected in its asking price. The most controversial topic relates to exactly what is a "from life photograph" of Lee (or anyone else). Of the many hundreds of Lee photographs available from dealers, collectors, and auction houses described as, or insinuated to be, "from life," only a handful were truly made from the negative produced as the General sat in front of the camera. Most by far are copies made later by one technique or another.

Q: *Where did you find the photographs for your book?*

A: Over the years I have accumulated for my own collection several Robert E. Lee photographs. In fact, detailed study of these photographs is what generated the spark of an idea for this book. Afterwards, I searched the well-known national repositories for Lee photographs as well as archival collections in museums, university libraries, and historical societies, copying photographs and noting their source. I also found a few in private collections but one of the more productive areas was in the catalogs of auction houses. A few photographs of Lee, unknown to me at the time, were found on internet sites. One of my more startling discoveries was on the wall of my own study. I had a framed photograph that I had owned for some time thinking it was simply a copy of a well-known image of Lee. As I studied its details, I learned that it was a virtually unknown photograph that had never been published! I wrote an article about it for *North South Trader's Civil War* magazine.

Q: *Where did you conduct your research?*

A: Much of my research was on site in Virginia at places like VMI, Washington and Lee University, The Museum of the Confederacy, The Virginia Historical Society, and The Valentine History Center. Other research was accomplished at the Mississippi Department of Archives and History and the Alabama Department of Archives and History. However, there is no question that most of my research hours were spent in front of my computer at home looking at websites, auction catalog

archives, current auctions, and dealer catalogs. I also learned a great deal in my email communications with interested scholars, dealers, and collectors.

Q: *What qualifies you to write what is basically a reference book on Robert E. Lee photographs?*

A: It is certainly not that I have any significant literary qualifications. I have written a couple of books including The Little Jeff: Jeff Davis Legion, Cavalry of the Army of Northern Virginia and Horsemen of the Jeff Davis Legion. I have written magazine articles, one about a Lee photograph and others medically related. I believe my best qualification for this project was that I recognized the inaccuracies and omissions throughout the available sources related to Robert E. Lee photographs and felt compelled to "set the record straight" to the best of my ability. My professional background as a physician who must pay attention to tiny details to be successful was also helpful. I consider myself an historical researcher first and a writer second.

Q: *Who will find your book most useful?*

A: When considering such a narrow subject as photographs of Robert E. Lee one instinctively assumes that it will appeal only to serious students of the subject, and certainly I expect this relatively small group to appreciate (and criticize) my book. I tried to broaden the interest by discussing photographic techniques of the period as well as photographers both north and south who took photographs of Lee or sold copies of his image. Those interested in 19th century photography and photographers should find it interesting and useful from this aspect. Those collectors and dealers who want accurate and up-to-date information about their Lee photographs as well as Civil War photographs in general should enjoy it. Finally, the layout and presentation of this book makes it suitable for a library collection or gracing the coffee table of anyone interested in the history of the South.

Q: *Do you consider your book to be the final word on Robert E. Lee photographs?*

A: Absolutely not. I do consider it the most complete and accurate study of the subject available today. I even have a chapter near the end which discusses four or five photographic sittings of Lee that at this time cannot definitively be placed as to time or place they were made; and there remains uncertainty as to the original photographer. This small collection discussed in the chapter entitled "Mysteries of Time and Place" will most certainly generate differing opinions among those interested in the topic and, as time goes by and with further study, concrete facts about these photographs will emerge.

Q: *Thank you for your time, we appreciate it.*

A: You're welcome.

BIBLIOGRAPHY
*consulted but not cited

Books

*Albaugh, William A., III. *Confederate Faces: Photographs of Confederates*. Wilmington, NC: Broadfoot Publishing Company, 1993.

*_____. *More Confederate Faces: Photographs of Confederates*. Wilmington, NC: Broadfoot Publishing Company, 1993.

Allen, Felicity. *Jefferson Davis, Unconquerable Heart*. Columbia, MO: University of Missouri Press, 1999.

*Baldwin, Gordon. *Looking at Photographs: A Guide to Technical Terms*. Malibu, CA: J. Paul Getty Museum, 1991.

Barber, James G., ed. *Faces of Discord: The Civil War Era at the National Portrait Gallery*. New York: Harper Collins Publisher, Smithsonian Institution, 2006.

*Bond, Christiana. *Memories of General Robert E. Lee*. Baltimore, MD: Norman, Remington Co., 1926.

Bostick, Douglas W. *The Confederacy's Secret Weapon: The Civil War Illustrations of Frank Vizetelly*. Charleston, SC: The History Press, 2009.

*Bradford, Gamaliel. *Lee the American*. Boston and New York: Houghton Mifflin Co., Riverside Press, Cambridge, 1912.

Carroll, John M. *List of Staff Officers of the Confederate States Army: With a New Introduction by John M. Carroll*, 1861-1865. Mattituck, NY: J. M. Carroll & Co., 1983.

Chambers, Lenoir. *Stonewall Jackson*. 1959. 2 vols. Wilmington, NC: Broadfoot Publishing Company, 1988.

*Chrysler Museum. *An Enduring Interest, the Photographs of Alexander Gardner*. Norfolk, VA: Teagle and Little, Inc., Printers, 1991.

City of Richmond, 1905; Of Historic Fame, of Great Commercial Prestige. [photographs by H. P. Cook]. Richmond, VA: Hermitage Press, 1905.

Confederate Veteran Magazine, 1893-1932. 40 vols. Wilmington, NC: Broadfoot Publishing Company, 1988.

*Couper, William, ed. *The Corps Forward: Biographical Sketches of the V.M.I. Cadets Who Fought at New Market*. Buena Vista, VA: Mariner Press, 2005.

*_____. *One Hundred Years at V.M.I.* Richmond, VA: Garrett and Massie, 1939.

Crawford, Barbara, and Royster Lyle. *Rockbridge County Artists and Artisans*. Charlottesville, VA: University of Virginia Press, 1995.

Dabney, Charles W. *Universal Education in the South*. 2 vols. Chapel Hill, NC: University of North Carolina Press, 1936.

Darrah, William C. *Cartes De Visite in Nineteenth Century Photography*. Gettysburg, PA: W. C. Darrah, 1981.

*Davis, William C., ed. *The Image of War, 1861-1865*. New York: Doubleday and Co., 1984.

Devine, William J. and Co., comp. *Richmond City Directory, 1866: Containing a business directory of all the persons engaged in business, classified according to the business: and a city register containing much useful information*. Richmond, VA: E. J. Townsend, 1866.

Dodds, Gordon, Roger Hall, and Stanley Triggs. *The World of William Notman: The Nineteenth Century through a Master Lens*. Boston, MA: David R. Godine, 1993.

Douglas, Henry Kyd. *I Rode with Stonewall*. Chapel Hill, NC: University of North Carolina Press, 1940.

Eicher, David J. *Robert E. Lee: A Life Portrait*. Dallas, TX: Taylor Publishing Co., 1997.

Emerson, B. A. C., comp. *Historic Southern Monuments: Representative Memorials of the Heroic Southern Dead of the Confederacy*. New York and Washington: Neale Publishing Co., 1911.

Ferslew, W. Eugene, comp. *First Annual Directory for the City of Richmond to which is added a Business Directory for 1859*. Richmond, VA: George W. West, 1859.

Fishwick, Marshall W. *General Lee's Photographer*. Chapel Hill, NC: University of North Carolina Press, published for Virginia Historical Society, 1957.

_____. *Lee after the War*. New York: Dodd, Mead and Co., 1963.

*Flood, Charles Bracelen. *Lee: The Last Years*. Boston, MA: Houghton Mifflin Co., 1981.

*Fralin, Frances. *The Indelible Images: Photographs of War – 1846 to the Present*. New York: Harry N. Abrams, 1985.

*Frassanito, William A. *Antietam: The Photographic Legacy of America's Bloodiest Day*. New York: Charles Scribner's Sons, 1978.

*_____. *Gettysburg: A Journey in Time*. New York: Charles Scribner's Sons, 1974.

*_____. *Grant and Lee: The Virginia Campaigns, 1864–1865*. New York: Charles Scribner's Sons, 1983.

Freeman, Douglas Southall. *R. E. Lee: A Biography*. 4 vols. New York and London: Charles Scribner's Sons, 1935.

*Gardner, Alexander. *Gardner's Photographic Sketch Book of the Civil War*. 1866. New York: Dover Publications, Inc., 1959.

*Ginsberg, Louis. *Photographers in Virginia, 1839-1900*. Petersburg, VA: L. Ginsberg, Publisher, 1986.

Hall, Charles B., comp. and illus. *Military Record of General Officers of the Confederate States of America*. 1898. Austin, TX: The Steck Co., 1963.

*Hobart, George. *Mathew Brady*. London: Macdonald & Co., 1984.

*Hoobler, Dorothy, and Thomas Hoobler. *Photographing History: The Career of Mathew Brady*. New York: G. P. Putnam's Sons, 1977.

*Horan, James D. *Mathew Brady: Historian with a Camera*. New York: Crown Publishers, 1955.

Jackson, Mary Anna. *Memoirs of Stonewall Jackson*. Louisville, KY: Prentice Press, Courier-Journal Job Printing Company, 1895.

*Johnson, Clint. *In the Footsteps of Jackson*. Winston-Salem, NC: John F. Blair, Publisher, 2002.

Jones, John William. *The Davis Memorial Volume: or, Our Dead President, Jefferson Davis and the World's Tribute to his Memory.* Richmond, VA: B. F. Johnson & Co, 1890.

*____. *Life and Letters of Robert E. Lee: Soldier and Man.* New York: Neal Publishing Co., 1906.

*____. *Personal Reminiscences, Anecdotes, and Letters: Gen. Robert E. Lee.* New York: D. Appleton, 1875.

Jones, John William, Robert Alonzo Brock, and James Power Smith, eds. *Southern Historical Society Papers, 1876-1959.* 52 vols. Millwood, NY: Kraus, 1977.

*Jones, T. *Illustrated Greetings from Richmond, Virginia.* [photographs by George S. Cook]. Cincinnati, OH: T. Jones, 1901.

Katcher, Philip. *American Civil War Armies (3): Staff, Specialist and Maritime Services.* London: Osprey Publishing Ltd., 1988.

Katz, Mark D. *Witness to an Era: The Life and Photographs of Alexander Gardner.* Nashville, TN: Rutledge Hill Press, 1991.

Kocher, A. Lawrence, and Howard Dearstyne. *Shadows in Silver: A Record of Virginia, 1850-1900, in Contemporary Photographs Taken by George and Huestis Cook, With Additions from the Cook Collection.* New York: Scribner, 1954.

*Kunhardt, Dorothy Meserve, and Philip B. Kunhardt, Jr. *Mathew Brady and His World.* Alexandria, VA: Time-Life Books, 1977.

Lattimore, Ralston B., ed. *The Story of Robert E. Lee as Told in his own Words and those of his Contemporaries.* Washington, D.C.: Colortone Press, 1964.

Lee, Robert E. *Recollections and Letters of General Lee, by His Son Captain Robert E. Lee.* New York: Garden City Publishing Co., 1926.

*Lewinski, Jorge. *The Camera at War: A History of War Photography from 1848 to the Present Day.* New York: Simon and Schuster, 1980.

*Lossing, Benson L. *Mathew Brady's Illustrated History of the Civil War.* New York: Fairfax Press, 1978.

*Marder, William, and Estelle Marder. *Anthony: The Man, the Company, the Camera.* Plantation, FL: Pine Ridge Publishing Co., 1982.

Meredith, Roy. *The Faces of Robert E. Lee in Life and in Legend.* Revised edition. New York: Fairfax Press, 1981.

Meredith, Roy. *Mr. Lincoln's Camera Man, Mathew Brady.* 2nd revised edition. New York: Dover Publications, Inc., 1974.

Milhollen, Hirst D., comp. *A Century of Photographs, 1846-1946.* Washington, D.C.: Library of Congress, 1980.

*____. *Civil War Photographs, 1861-1865.* Washington, D.C.: Library of Congress, 1977.

Miller, Francis Trevelyan, ed. *The Photographic History of the Civil War, Thousands of Scenes Photographed 1861-65, with Text by many Special Authorities.* 10 vols. New York: The Review of Reviews Co., 1912.

Monckhoven, D. van, trans. W. H. Thorntwaite. *A Popular Treatise on Photography also a Description of, and Remarks on, the Stereoscope and Photographic Optics, Etc. Etc.,* London: Virtue Brothers, 1863.

*Morton, Oren F. *A History of Rockbridge County, Virginia*. Staunton, VA: The McClure Co., 1920.

Neely, Mark E., Jr., and Harold Holzer. *The Lincoln Family Album: Photographs from the Personal Collection of a Historic American Family*. New York: Doubleday, 1990.

Neely, Mark E., Jr., Harold Holzer, and Gabor S. Boritt. *The Confederate Image: Prints of the Lost Cause*. Chapel Hill, NC: University of North Carolina Press, 2000.

Palmquist, Peter E., ed. *The Daguerreian Annual 1990: Official Yearbook of the Daguerreian Society*. Eureka, CA: Eureka Printing Company, Inc., 1990.

*Palmquist, Peter E., and Thomas R. Kailbourn. *Pioneer Photographers from the Mississippi to the Continental Divide*. Stanford, CA: Stanford University Press, 2005.

Pendleton, Robert M. *Traveller: General Robert E. Lee's Favorite Greenbrier War Horse*. Victoria, British Columbia, Canada: Trafford, 2005.

Ramsay, Jack C., Jr. *Photographer – Under Fire: The Story of George S. Cook (1819-1902)*. Green Bay, WI: Historical Resources Press, 1994.

*Reilly, James M. *Care and Identification of 19th Century Photographic Prints*. Rochester, NY: Silver Pixel Press, 1986.

Riley, Franklin L., ed. *General Robert E. Lee after Appomattox*. New York: McMillan Company, 1922.

*Rinehart, Floyd, and Marian Rinehart. *The American Daguerreotype*. Athens, GA: The University of Georgia Press, 1981.

Ruggles, Jeffery. *Photography in Virginia*. Richmond, VA: Virginia Historical Society, 2008.

*Russell, Andrew J. *Russell's Civil War Photographs*. New York: Dover Publishing, 1982.

*Serrano, D. A. *Still More Confederate Faces*. Bayside, NY: Metropolitan Co., 1992.

*Severn, Joan. *Dressed for the Photographer*. Kent, OH: Kent State University Press, 1995.

Stern, Philip Van Doren. *Robert E. Lee, the Man and the Soldier*. New York: Bonanza Books, 1963.

*Sweet, Timothy. *Traces of War: Poetry, Photography, and the Crisis of the Union*. Baltimore, MD: Johns Hopkins University Press, 1990.

Teal, Harry S. *Partners with the Sun: South Carolina Photographers, 1840-1940*. Columbia, SC: University of South Carolina Press, 2001.

Thomas, Emory M. *Robert E. Lee: An Album*. New York and London: W. W. Norton and Co., 2000.

*Trachtenberg, Alan. *Reading American Photographs: Images as History, Mathew Brady to Walker Evans*. New York: Hill and Wang, 1989.

Turner, William. *Even More Confederate Faces*. Gaithersburg, MD: Olde Soldier Books, Inc., 1993.

Valentine, Elizabeth Gray. *Dawn to Twilight: Work of Edward V. Valentine*. Richmond, VA: William Byrd Press, Inc., 1929.

*Wayland, John W. *Robert E. Lee and His Family*. Staunton, VA.: The McClure Printing Company, 1951.

*White, Henry Alexander. *Robert E. Lee and the Southern Confederacy, 1807-1870*. New York: G. P. Putnam and Sons, 1897.

*Willoughby, Laura E. *Petersburg, Then and Now*. Charleston, SC: Arcadia Publishing, 2010.

Wise, John Sergeant. *The End of an Era*. Boston and New York: Houghton Mifflin Co., Riverside Press, Cambridge, 1899.

*Witham, George F., comp. *Catalog of Civil War Photographers: A Listing of Civil War Photographers' Imprints*. Portland, OR: G. F. Witham, 1988.

*Zeller, Bob. *The Blue and Gray in Black and White: A History of Civil War Photography*. Westport, CT: Praeger, 2005.

Periodicals

Anthony, E. and H. T. Advertisement. *Harper's Weekly*, November 7, 1863, 720.

"Bendann Brothers' Backgrounds." *Photographic Times*, May 1872, 69.

Briggs, Martha Wren. "The Camera-Shy General." *The United Daughters of the Confederacy Magazine*, March 1994, 18-19.

*Bryan, Thomas Conn. "General William J. Hardee and Confederate Publication Rights." *The Journal of Southern History* 12, no. 2 (May 1946): 263-274.

*Campbell, Edward D. C. "The Fabric of Command: R. E. Lee, Confederate Insignia, and the Perception of Rank." *The Virginia Magazine of History and Biography*, April 1980, 261-290.

Clark, John, ed. "The Photographic Art." *The Norfolk [VA] Post*, July 21, 1865, 2.

"Daguerreotypy." *Photographic Times and American Photographer*, June 7, 1889, 279-281.

D. H. Anderson. Advertisement. *Southern Planter and Farmer*, January 1870, 27.

Frishman, Bob. "Mathew Brady's Clock." *National Association of Watch and Clock Collectors' Bulletin*, October 2002, 605.

"Gen. Lee in Baltimore," *The Daily News* [Lynchburg, VA], February 15, 1866.

Hopkins, Donald. "A New Image of Lee." *North South Trader's Civil War: A Magazine for Collectors & Historians*, March-April 2004, 36-40.

Katz, Mark D. "New Faces of Robert E. Lee." *Civil War Times Illustrated*, April 1983, 42-45.

"Nation's Most Famous Historical Photograph Identified." *The Lexington [VA] Gazette*, August 21, 1935.

O'Brien, John. "Brady and Lee: 1866, The History of a Photographic Session," *Military Images Magazine*, March-April 1986, 6-8.

O'Donnell, Mike, and Steve Sylvia. "Unknown Lee Photo Found!" *North South Trader*, September-October 1985, 29.

*Parker, Franklin. "R. E. Lee, George Peabody, and Sectional Reunion." *Peabody Journal of Education* [1960] 78, no. 1, reprint (January 2003): 91-97.

Richmond [VA] Daily Dispatch. Various, November 1860-December 1865.

"Robert Edmund [sic] Lee." *Harper's Weekly*, July 2, 1864, 1.

Sampson, H. "Making Enlarged Negatives from Small Ones." *The Professional and Amateur Photographer*, vol. 5, September 1900, 340-343.

Smith, Everard H., ed. "As They Saw General Lee." *Civil War Times Illustrated*, October 1986, 20-23.

Tennant, T. Dixon. "Editor's Table." *Wilson's Photographic Magazine*, March 1909, 144.

Wilson, Edward L., ed. "Our Picture." *Philadelphia Photographer* 2, no. 22 (October 1865): 170.

Archived Material

Carte de visite Photograph, Robert E. Lee in Civilian Dress. Museum and photograph record, 2001.2.140. Virginia Historical Society. Richmond, VA.

Dooley, Edwin L., Jr. *Transcribed, Corrected, and Annotated. 1860 Census Town of Lexington, Virginia*. Virginia Military Institute Archives, 2008. Lexington, VA.

"Explanatory Statement concerning Rees & Co. Photograph of Robert E. Lee, 1956." Accession #5457. University of Virginia Library. Charlottesville, VA.

George S. and H. Cook Papers, 1912-1925, 1929. Manuscript Collection No. 28. Valentine Richmond History Center. Richmond, VA.

Harwell, Richard. "Illustrated Typescript Note." Museum Collection. *Virginia Historical Society*. Richmond, VA.

History of the Photograph. Old typescript note attached to back of original, 1870s period, framed photograph. Hopkins Collection. Gulfport, MS.

"Lee Collections." *Lee-Jackson Foundation Letters Transcriptions*. Special Collections and Archives. Leyburn Library. Washington and Lee University. Lexington, VA.

"Lee Collections." *Letters of the Lee Family Transcriptions*. Special Collections and Archives. Leyburn Library. Washington and Lee University. Lexington, VA.

"Lee Collections." *Robert E. Lee Letters Transcriptions*. Special Collections and Archives. Leyburn Library. Washington and Lee University. Lexington, VA.

Lee, Robert E., Probably the Last Photograph. Negative No. 5023-A'23. Dementi Studio Archives. Richmond, VA.

Mary Custis Lee to Edward V. Valentine, September 29, 1870. Manuscript Collection 57. Valentine Richmond History Center. Richmond, VA.

Miley, Henry. *Oral Recollections*, 1941 (typescript). Special Collections and Archives. Leyburn Library. Washington and Lee University. Lexington, VA.

"Mr. Peabody and His Friends (scrapbook)." *George Peabody Papers*. Peabody Institute Library Papers. Peabody, ME.

Robert E. Lee with Fincastle Wartime Girls. Museum No. 2001.2.31. Virginia Historical Society. Richmond, VA.

"Untitled Tabulation in E. V. Valentine's Hand." Manuscript Collection 57. Valentine Richmond History Center. Richmond, VA.

Pamphlets, Circulars, Catalogs

*Broadfoot, Thomas W. *Civil War, Catalog 130*. Wendell, NC: Broadfoot's Bookmark, 1983.

*Simpson, Pamela, and Mame Warren. *Michael Miley, American Photographer and Pioneer in Color*. Exhibition catalog. Lexington, VA: Washington and Lee University, 1980.

Statutes at Large of the Confederate States of America Passed at the Third Session of the First Congress. Richmond, VA: R.M. Smith, 1863.

United States. *United States Copyright Office: A Brief History*. Circular 1a. Washington, D.C.: U.S. Government Copyright Office, 2008.

*Wilson, Joseph M. *A Eulogy on the Life and Character of Alexander Gardner*. Washington, D.C.: R. Beresford, 1883.

Auction Catalogs

Cowan's Auctions. "Fine Unpublished, Autographed CDV of Robert E. Lee," catalog entry. *Historic Americana Auction*. Cincinnati, OH: Cowan's Auctions, Inc., 2005.

_____. "Libby Prison Presentation Photograph from a New Jersey Officer," catalog entry. *Western and Historical Americana*. Cincinnati, OH: Cowan's Auctions, Inc., 2009.

_____. "Robert E. Lee and Confederate Generals at White Sulphur Springs, WV, Plus," catalog entry. *American History Including the Civil War*. Cincinnati, OH: Cowan's Auctions, Inc., 2011.

_____. "Scarce Unpublished 1867 Rees Photograph of Robert E. Lee," catalog entry. *Historic Americana Auction*. Cincinnati, OH: Cowan's Auctions, Inc., 2008.

Heritage Auctions. "Autograph Letter Signed by Robert E. Lee accompanied by a Signed Carte De Viste of the General in a Confederate Uniform," catalog entry. *June 2007 Civil War Grand Format Auction*. Gettysburg, PA: Heritage Auctions, 2007.

_____. "Robert E. Lee Carte De Visite," catalog entry. *Manuscripts Grand Format Auction*. New York: Heritage Auctions, 2011.

_____. "Robert E. Lee Carte de Visite signed R.E. Lee," catalog entry. *2008 November Signature Civil War Auction*. Dallas, TX: Heritage Auctions, 2008.

_____. "Sculptor Edward Valentine's Personal Vannerson Photographs of Robert E. Lee Used in Modeling his Famous Statue," catalog entry. *Civil War Grand Format Auction*. Dallas, TX: Heritage Auctions, 2007.

Raynor's Historical Collectible Auctions. Catalog Archives. Burlington, NC: 1995-2011.

Swann Galleries. "Portrait of Robert E. Lee; Salt Print, Mtd," catalog entry. *Important 19th and 20th Century Photographs*. New York: Swann Galleries, Inc., 2000.

Internet Sites

"Augusta County Fair." *Staunton [VA] Spectator*. November 10, 1868. http://www2.vcdh.virginia.edu/saxon/servle/

Bendann, Lance. *History* [of Bendann's Art Gallery]. http://www.bendannartgalleries.com/BendannHistory.htm

Bently, Lionel, and Martin Kretschmer, eds. "Confederate States of America Copyright Act (1861)." *Primary Sources on Copyright (1450-1900)*. Ithaca, NY: Cornell University Law Library, 2011. http://www.copyrighthistory.org

Broomall, James J. "Photography During the Civil War." *Encyclopedia Virginia*. Ed. Brendan Wolfe. Virginia Foundation for the Humanities, 2011. http://www.EncyclopediaVirginia.org/Photography_During_the_Civil_War.

"Building in the Burnt District of Richmond." *The Norfolk Post*. July 13, 1865. http://chroniclingamerica.com

"City Directories for Southside Hampton Roads." Norfolk, VA: Norfolk Public Library. http://www.npl.lib.va.us/SMRT/City_Directories.html

"Confederates and their Liverpool Connections," *When Liverpool went Dixie*. http://www.bbc.co.uk/liverpool/localhistory/journey/american_connection/alabama/bulloch_liverpool.shtml

Craig, John S. *Craig's Daguerreian Registry: The Acknowledged Resource on American Photographers 1839-1860.* http://craigcamera.com/dag

"Father, Daughter Dead." *[Richmond, VA] Times Dispatch*, December 8, 1903. http://chroniclingamerica.loc.gov

"Gilder Lehrman Collection." Gilder Lehrman Institute of American History. New York. http://www.gilderlehrman.org/collections

Gorman, Michael D. "Civil War Richmond." Richmond, VA: Civil War Richmond, Inc., 2008. http://www.mdgorman.com/Photographs

____. "Civil War Richmond." Richmond, VA: Civil War Richmond, Inc., 2008. http://www.mdgorman.com/Written_Accounts/newspaper

____. "Lee the 'Devil' Discovered at Images of War Seminar: Derisive Graffiti Appears in 1865 Brady Photo of Lee." *Center for Civil War Photography Newsletter*. February 2006. http://www.civilwarphotography.org/index.php/newsletters/117-volume-4-issue-1-february-2006#LeeDevil

Hirtle, Peter. *Copyright Term and the Public Domain in the United States*. Cornell University Copyright Information Center. Cornell University Library, 2011. http://copyright.cornell.edu/resources/publicdomain.cfm

"It-Kha-Ka-Hang-Zhe, Standing Elk, Warrior, Yankton Sioux." Chrysler Museum Collection, Object No. 9235. Norfolk, VA. http://collectiononline.chrysler.org/emuseum/view/objects/asitem/People

"List of Premiums Awarded at the Seventh Annual exhibition of the Virginia Mechanic's Institute, which Closed on the Night of the 31st ct., 1860." *Richmond Daily Dispatch*. November 1, 1860. http://dlxs.richmond.edu/d/ddr

Norfolk and Portsmouth Business Directory, 1875-76. http://www.npl.lib.va.us/smrt/directories/1875-1876NorfPort

Parsons, Ralph. "Linoleum: A Chiswick Invention." *Brentford Chiswick Local History Journal*. Journal 5, 1996. http://brentfordandchiswicklhs.org.uk/local-history/industries-and-crafts/linoleum-a,-chiswick-invention/

"The Photographic Art." *The Norfolk Post*. July 21, 1865. http://chroniclingamerica.loc.gov/lccn/

Pryor, Elizabeth Brown. "Mary Anna Randolph Custis Lee (1807–1873)." Encyclopedia Virginia. Ed. Brendan Wolfe. Virginia Foundation for the Humanities. January 14, 2012. http://www.encyclopediavirginia.org/Lee_Mary_Anna_Randolph_Custis_1807-1873.

"Richmond Daily Dispatch, 1860-1865." Institute of Museum and Library Services. University of Richmond, Tufts University, and Virginia Center for Digital History. 2003. http://dlxs.richmond.edu/d/ddr

"Sent to Fort Lafayette, from the *Baltimore Sun*, July 11, 1862." *New York Times*. July 16, 1862. http://query.nytimes.com/gst/abstract.html

"Through the Lens of Time." Digital Collections, Special Collections and Archives. Virginia Commonwealth University. Richmond, VA. http://dig.library.vcu.edu/cdm/landing-page/collection/cook

"Untitled article." *Richmond [VA] Daily Whig*. August 20, 1869, p. 3, c. 2. http://bf-parker.blog.co.uk/2011/10/18/14-of-14-george-peabody-1795-1869-a-z-handbook-of-the-massachusetts-born-merchant-in-the-south-london-based-banker-and-philanthropist-s-life-infl-12030377

Uriguen, Mikel. "Civil War Generals in Black and White." *General and Brevets*. http://www.generalsandbrevets.com/sgl/leere11.htm

INDEX

ABOUT THE AUTHOR

Born in the rural South, Donald A. Hopkins has maintained a fascination with Southern history since he was a child. In addition to published papers in the medical field, he has written several Civil War articles and *The Little Jeff: The Jeff Davis Legion, Cavalry, Army of Northern Virginia* for which he received the United Daughters of the Confederacy's Jefferson Davis Historical Gold Medal. Dr. Hopkins is a surgeon in Gulfport, Mississippi, where he lives with his wife Cindy and their golden retriever Dixie.